COLUMBIA UNIVERSITY LECTURES

CONSTITUTIONAL POWER AND WORLD AFFAIRS

BY

GEORGE SUTHERLAND
FORMER UNITED STATES SENATOR FROM UTAH

𝕹𝖊𝖜 𝔜𝖔𝖗𝖐

COLUMBIA UNIVERSITY PRESS

1919

CONTENTS

CHAPTER I

THE GREAT WAR—DEMOCRACY AND THE CONSTITUTION

For four years the world has been swept and tossed by a great storm of human passion. Until very recently the only thing of which we could be certain was that the storm would pass and the sun of peace again appear; but when and under what circumstances, we could only guess. At last the skies have cleared and the end has come.

In the natural world when the rain has ceased and the winds have fallen we look about to see what monarchs of the forest have been up-rooted; what new channels have been torn in the soil by flood and torrent along which the peaceful streams may thereafter flow. In the same way with the end of this war we may, with profit, look about us for the purpose of approximating the changes which have been wrought in the world, and the meaning and effect of these changes so far as we are ourselves concerned. In the midst of it, with the end in doubt, all we could foresee was that the familiar world which we had known and understood would forever pass away, and that a new and different world would be spread before our vision. Whether it was to be a worse world has at length been removed from the realm of uncertainty, and it has been made sure that because of the triumph of the ideals for which we have been fighting, it has fallen to ourselves and our allies to make it a far better world than we have ever known.

When the struggle began we were filled with horror and bewilderment. It was difficult to determine what it was all about. But as time passed we saw, at first dimly and then with great clearness, that it was not a contest between contending armies alone, or between contending nations or peoples alone; but that the underlying causes were to be found in the antagonisms of two opposing political systems, teaching irreconcilable doctrines: one that sovereignty—the plenary power to determine all questions of government without accountability to any one—is in the people and nowhere else; the other that sovereignty is a king's chattel to be handed down from father to son. The first view is embodied in the words of the American Declaration of Independence, that "governments are instituted among men deriving their just powers from the consent of the governed." The other view has been nowhere more happily expressed than by the late German Kaiser himself in a speech delivered before the war, in which he is reported to have said: "You Germans have only one will and that is my will; you have only one law and that is my law; there is but one master in this country and I am he, and whoever opposes me I will crush into pieces."

In the last analysis it was against this brutal and arrogant conception of personal and autocratic sovereignty that the free peoples of the world set themselves to the grim business of war. The character of the parties arrayed against one another gave additional emphasis to the nature of the issue. Upon one side there was heroic Belgium with bloody but unbowed head; liberty-loving Italy; beloved France, land of liberty, equality and fraternity; sturdy, stubborn England, home of religious and political tolerance, birth-place of Anglo-Saxon liberty; and, finally, *and almost too late*, America, land of the "free hearts' hope and home," whose gates have always swung inward to the oppressed of every other land. Upon the other side there were Germany, whose master was the Kaiser; Austria, whose master was the Emperor; Turkey, whose master was the Sultan. In short, nearly all the peoples of the earth whose rulers were their servants stood finally in battle-line against nearly all the peoples of the earth whose rulers were their masters. Into this gigantic maelstrom a billion people were precipitated until substantially the whole civilized world became involved. The face of Europe has been drenched with blood and made a place of indescribable horror. The eye, turning in any direction, beheld only the somber and terrifying clouds of war. The struggle has been so titanic that adjectives have become meaningless. Recorded history furnishes no parallel. Past wars have shrunk to the dimensions of insignificance. The campaigns of Alexander, of Caesar, of Napoleon, dwindle by comparison to the proportions of neighborhood riots. Armed forces so great, a battlefield so vast, issues so momentous have never existed since the legions of darkness were overthrown by the legions of light, and "hurled headlong" from the crystal battlements into the infernal pit.

A few months ago when the German armies were pressing swiftly toward Paris there came to us a vivid and uncomfortable realization of the dangers we were facing. Democracy we knew was righteous, but we were confronted with the appalling possibility that it might not be efficient; and we were called upon, at whatsoever cost, to strengthen it or perish; for of what avail is righteousness if it cannot be preserved from destruction?

Let it be said to our credit that the faint-hearted among us were few. Instinctively we had faith; and we never doubted that somehow in the end there would spring not a foul weed but a lovely flower from the blood-soaked soil of France and Flanders.

That Germany has lost and civilization has won, has been as much due to German blunders as to Allied skill and courage. If her higher strategy and diplomacy had been equal to her military strength, the world would now have a German master. For forty years, as we now know, she coldly plotted this war. She builded and perfected a military machine that seemed invincible. Her plans, skillfully drawn, were apparently flawless. By all the rules of military mathematics there was no physical power able to stand against her. But the factor which finally determines in human affairs is the imponderable, and Germany forgot there was a human soul. She knew Belgium was small and weak, but she did not realize that the soul of Belgium was unconquerable. The bodies of Englishmen she knew were untrained, but she should have remembered that the English spirit had been disciplined in the school of battle for a thousand years. She looked upon us as a nation of money grubbers who cared for nothing but our own ease, and did not know that we loved justice more than we hated war. And so Belgium fought almost with bare hands; England welded her raw levies into

armies of invincible soldiers; Italy drew the sword;
and at last America became an armed camp from which
millions of her young men have poured forth to battle.
From Switzerland to the sea the men of France, Belgium, Italy, Great Britain and America builded of their
own bodies a living wall of flesh against which the
veteran armies of the Central Powers beat in vain until
at last the wall became a flood and swept back toward
the Rhine those whom it did not engulf.

It has been no holiday enterprise in which we have
been engaged, but stern and deadly business; for this
was the alternative we faced—this and no lesser thing
—that either we must destroy military Germany or
military Germany would destroy us. Under the circumstances we would have been guilty of black treason
to have kept out of the war; treason to everything
which we were bound to hold sacred; treason to the
millions of brave men who have died upon land and
sea for a cause that was also our cause; treason to the
millions of hopelessly maimed who will never know the
full joys of life again; treason to the suffering souls of
thousands of good women who have been unspeakably
wronged; treason to the murdered children of Europe
and to our own, a vision of whose white, dead faces,
tossing upon a cold sea and upturned to the stars, would
never have ceased to be a haunting and unanswerable
reproach. I, for one, shall never cease to thank God
that we escaped from this abhorrent plight while yet
there was time.

For two years and a half we deluded ourselves with
the fiction that the war was exclusively a European
affair in which we had nothing more than a sentimental

interest.   Belgium was invaded, her towns pillaged and
destroyed, her people outraged, enslaved, murdered.
We closed the ears of our reason to the sinister threat
which this conduct implied against our own liberties
and possessions.   We shut the eyes of our imagination
and would not see the dark shadow which it cast over
the possible future of our own land.   Belgium was
thought to be protected by formal treaty.   She was
without offense even against Germany, save that she
objected to the use of her territory as a military highway for the passage of German armies on their way to
a swift defeat of France, and thereby refused to become
a criminal accomplice in an attack upon a friendly
neighbor, who was, moreover, one of the guarantors
of her neutrality.   The treaty guaranteeing Belgium's
neutrality became a "scrap of paper" and the arm of
Belgium, raised in just opposition to an atrocious tres-
pass, was stricken down with brutal circumstance as
though it had been lifted not in self-defense but against
God's anointed.   Not only this, but, in an effort to
justify the wanton and brutal assault, Germany afterward assailed and falsely impugned the good faith of
her victim—as outrageous a proceeding as though an
individual, having made an attack upon a pure woman,
should seek to excuse himself by circulating vile slanders
against her good name.

The violation of the neutrality of Luxembourg,
though not followed by the same tragic consequences,
was, in its inception, worse than the violation of Belgium.   The neutrality of Luxembourg was not only
guaranteed by a treaty to which Prussia was a party
in 1867, and which had been categorically recognized as

binding by and upon the German Empire, but the Duchy was *prohibited from arming itself for its own defense*. Thus the invasion was not only a gross breach of the solemn obligation to which the German government was pledged, but it was a wicked assault upon a weak and utterly defenseless people, as contemptible and cowardly as the assault of a powerful bully upon a defenseless child.

And so the temper and purpose of Germany stood revealed. Pledges were no longer binding, treaties were no longer sacred, international faith was a lie, possession of anything which Germany wanted was *casus belli*, and the rights of the weak or defenseless were to be measured by Prussian needs and might. Every consideration of humanity and chivalry called for an indignant protest upon our part against these cynical and bloody violations of international decency. But laying this aside, we were ourselves gravely, yea, vitally, concerned, because the incidents constituted clear warning that a wild beast was at large from whose rage we were no more immune than was Belgium. When Belgium was invaded we should have remembered that Mexico lay along our southern flank as Belgium lay along the northern flank of France, and if we did not condemn the use of neutralized Belgium to attack France, the day might come when France and the friends of France might look with small concern upon the use of the territory of a neutral Mexico through which to attack us.

Finally, we became ourselves the victims of direct aggression. Our ships were sunk and our citizens murdered upon the high seas and we were arrogantly informed that we might travel that common highway of all nations only upon such humiliating conditions as Germany saw fit to impose. Even then a large body of our people favored a continuation of the weak and dangerous policy of diplomatic negotiation. They shrank before the inevitable and even insisted—some of them— that we had no power to send an army overseas, but must await an actual invasion of our own soil before resorting to armed force. They were utterly wrong, of course, for the Constitution contemplates *offensive*, as well as *defensive* warfare, since it recognizes not only the power to *repel invasions* but confers the power to *declare war*. It was never intended that peace at any price should become the policy of a people whose very independence was *forced* at the point of the sword.

An individual having only himself to consider may act in conformity to his personal taste. If he choose the course of non-resistance to physical aggression, however intolerable, that is his own affair, and it is not without the sanction of high authority, though the justification would depend, I should think, upon whether the non-resistance were the result of high principle or of cowardice—dictated by one's own free choice or by the imposed will of another. That it is better to suffer wrong than to do wrong is a sentiment of such obvious truth and nobility as to be beyond question, but it does not follow that it is better to suffer wrong than to resist it. If it be righteous to passively submit to aggression when only the wrong-doer and the wronged are concerned, or, to go even further and turn the other cheek, I am afraid I am hopelessly heterodox; for it seems to me far better to fight wrong with all one's strength, though directed against one's self alone, until the wrong-doer has been lain in the dust or one can fight no more. Even in matters of purely personal concern I should turn the other cheek with the greatest possible reluctance.

But whatever may be the ethics of the matter in the case of the individual, the government of a self-respecting people should be swayed by no such sentiment. The individual represents only himself; but the government is a trustee, wielding the power and safeguarding the rights of those who created and continue it. If those in control of the government yield to the aggressor, they do not yield their own; they betray the trust. The Golden Rule in such case is: "Do not suffer others to do unto you what you should not do unto them." *Think of the tragic consequences to the world if brave Belgium had turned the other cheek!*

This struggle in which we have been engaged in so large a way the world has witnessed in a small way many times. Sometimes victory has favored one view and sometimes the other, but in the aggregate of the last century and a half of history the balance greatly preponderates in favor of the popular side. When the American Declaration of Independence was written one could live nowhere except among a king-ridden people. There had been occasional gleams of light but no country had beheld the risen sun. Until 1776 no people had been found bold enough to deny that the powers of government were derived from the consent of the ruler, albeit from time to time the denial of an occasional individual had been recorded. Men of courageous soul had faced the King and compelled his

reluctant recognition of certain fundamental conceptions of popular liberty. Magna Charta, the Petition
of Right, the Bill of Rights, and other charters of
English liberty had been grudgingly granted by the
Kings of England. The lasting importance of these
concessions cannot be overestimated. They constitute
the footing-stones of individual rights today—the common heritage of Anglo-Saxons everywhere. But the
significant fact is that they *were* concessions made by
the King, and not rights recognized as inherent in the
people which no king had the power to withhold. The
very fact that they were wrung from the King was a
recognition that the King and not the people constituted their source. If their existence depended upon
the royal *grant* even though compelled by the people
against the royal *wish*, it logically follows that the ultimate repository of power was the governor and not
the governed.

The American Revolution, however, proceeded upon
the principle that sovereignty belongs to the people,
and it is by their consent, either express or implied,
that the governing agency acts in any particular way,
or acts at all. This is the animating principle of the
Declaration of Independence. It is the very soul of
the Constitution, which at once proclaims and bears
witness to the fact that ultimate power resides only
with the people. It has become the fashion in some cir-
cles to denounce the written Constitution as undemo-
cratic, as an unwarranted restraint upon the freedom
of the people to move forward; but in truth it is the
most democratic thing we possess, for it is the one thing
above all other things that makes articulate and clear

the claim that all political power comes from the people. It is the one thing above all other things that makes the government which it establishes a servant of the people and prevents it from becoming their master; for it is the supreme law by which the people affirm their sovereignty and constitute their agents to exercise it to such extent, and in such form, as they decree. It speaks the language of paramount authority: "We, the people . . . do ordain and establish this Constitution for the United States of America." In the stately phrase of Webster: "It is the people's Constitution, the people's government, made for the people and answerable to the people."

The limitations of the Constitution are not bonds which fetter the people; they are restraints imposed by the people themselves upon the government which they have created as an instrumentality through which they rule in order that their creature may never forget that it has a creator. Even in democratic England, where the King may do anything he likes except rule, and the popular will as expressed by the majority generally prevails, sovereignty does not rest in the people but in Parliament; and indeed for all practical purposes not in Kings, Lords and Commons, but in the House of Commons alone. Parliament may do anything. There is no limit to its political power. There is no such thing as a completely sovereign English people, or if there be, it is only in a highly theoretical sense, for, practically speaking, Parliament is omnipotent, sovereign, without limitation or qualification. The outstanding difference between the traditional English Constitution and our written Constitution is, therefore, that the former estab-

lishes no restraint upon Parliament, while the latter is
an ever-sounding proclamation that the people's sovereignty has not been abandoned to any department of
the government or to all departments combined, but
only *delegated* in certain specified particulars. And the
Ninth and Tenth Amendments declare: "The enumeration in the Constitution of certain rights shall not be
construed to deny or disparage others retained by the
people;" "The powers not delegated to the United
States . . . are reserved to the States respectively
or to the people." To destroy the Constitution would,
therefore, be to destroy this high evidence that ultimate sovereignty remains with the people, that the
government is a mere instrumentality which exists for
the sake of the people instead of the people existing
for the sake of the government, and, moreover, as the
Fathers thought, to open the door of opportunity for
stealthy appropriations of power on the part of our
governmental agencies which might finally reach dangerous proportions. And so I repeat, for the sake of
emphasis, that the Constitution is the most democratic
of our possessions, democratic in every phrase and
sentence, for in every phrase and sentence it speaks
the will of the people, those who made it and ratified
it in the beginning, those who have maintained it and
added to it since, and those whose will it speaks today
and whose will it must continue to speak until they,
in the exercise of their sovereign authority, see fit to
put something else in its place.

The Constitution is, of course, not perfect. The makers themselves did not so consider it, since they provided for its alteration and extension by amendment.

One of its great virtues is that it *fixes* the rules by which we are to govern and by which we are to be governed. The value of a settled rule of conduct is not alone that men may be compelled to do justice; it is also that they may know *what* they are to do, and *how* they are to do it. Hence the justice and wisdom of the rule and its certainty are almost, and sometimes quite, of equal importance. I have, for example, no doubt that a much larger proportion of the decisions of courts are wrong than is generally suspected; but a decision right or wrong, settles the case, and very often settles the question as well. The parties concerned know what they may or may not do in the future. Even if the decision be wrong the doctrine of *res judicata* prevents any change which will affect the immediate cause, and the doctrine of *stare decisis* constrains the courts to follow it in other cases unless the vice of the decision be pretty clearly apparent. Thus much of principle we may be called upon to sacrifice to the advantage of stability. If it be so important to stabilize the decisions of courts which may affect only one's pocket-book or one's property, how much more important is it to stabilize those great principles of government and of liberty which lie at the foundation of the social structure!

There are two ways of stabilizing these fundamental principles: by the force of, and common respect for, long continued custom which is advisory, and by formal convention which is compelling. The former is illustrated by the Constitution of Great Britain, and the latter by the American Constitution.

We hear it said, sometimes, that our desires to work out new and enlarged conceptions of social justice are constantly thwarted by the restraining limitations of our Constitution, and it is impatiently suggested that if Great Britain can get along safely and more expeditiously under an advisory Constitution there is no reason why our progress should be impeded by the restrictions of a mandatory Constitution. But the cases are not parallel. The English Constitution is the result of many centuries of slow development. It has grown as the people and their institutions have grown, "bone of their bones and flesh of their flesh." It is not a force acting *upon* the various instrumentalities of government, but a force *of and within* them. It molds and directs their conduct by inward admonition rather than by outward compulsion. It is not an ordinance like the American Constitution, establishing and limiting political institutions, but a spirit which accompanied the development of these institutions and grew with them, and constitutes in a very real sense their expression and interpretation.

Regard for and obedience to the British Constitution by the governmental agencies of Great Britain are instinctive and habitual—not because it is so ordered, but because it is the thing to do. Failure or refusal would be followed by no positive consequences; everybody simply would be more or less shocked.

At the conclusion of the Revolutionary struggle, however, we found ourselves a nation of people with no common and traditional polity. The American Nation did not grow as the British Nation grew, from small beginnings and little by little. It sprang into full maturity at once. As a political society it could not endure without a constitution of government, and having none by growth it was obliged to make one by contrivance and construction.

An illustration may help to make clear the distinction. Suppose four or five adventurous explorers should come together in a new country and find themselves its sole occupants. They would readily arrive at an understanding, without formality or writing, of the few simple rules necessary for the regulation of their intercourse. Other persons joining them from time to time, there would be, perhaps at the end of a long period, a large and constantly augmenting population. Under these conditions, the political and social institutions of the country, and the fundamental principles regulating their relations to the people, would take form and develop by insensible degrees. The process would be like the movement of the large hands of a clock which we never see, and which we perceive from time to time only by comparison after the movement has taken place.

On the other hand, let us suppose that a multitude of people suddenly found themselves without political institutions and governing rules. The impossibility of informal understandings would be apparent, and their only escape from disorder and chaos would be to adopt a system of rules which, to avoid future dispute and misunderstanding, must be set down in explicit terms. The difference is between a polity which has grown and a polity which has been made. Our written Constitution was, therefore, the original and necessary means of giving expression and sanction to the fundamental law of the land and of establishing governmental institutions; and it must remain not only for this purpose but as at once the tie and the indispensable evidence of the

tie which holds the states in the bonds of indestructible
and perpetual union.

But though the Constitution stabilizes the principles
of government, it does not fix or define these principles
minutely or in detail.   The powers of government are
conferred in broad, general terms.   They are, as it has
been frequently said, not defined but enumerated; and
this enumeration is more frequently in the nature of a
statement of the *subjects* to which the powers of government apply than an enumeration of the *powers* themselves.   The authority of the several departments of
government is, therefore, of great flexibility.   The Constitution was intended to be perpetual and hence to
cover the changing needs of the people and the country,
the extent of which changes were within the contemplation but not within the knowledge of the framers.
Within the broad limits of the enumerated subjects it
was intended that power should keep pace with need,
and that the Constitution should be the source of this
power as a spring is the ever living source of an ever
flowing stream and not as a cistern is the source of a
precisely measured and rigidly limited supply.

The close of the Revolution and the subsequent adoption of the Constitution found us with the idea of popular sovereignty firmly established as the fundamental
principle of our political system.   We were, however, in
doubt as to the exact nature of the system itself.   Had
we created a Federation or a Nation?   The question
was the subject of controversy, always earnest and
sometimes exceedingly bitter, for more than half a
century.   Until the Civil War, the Union was a theory
for debate—to be vigorously denied and passionately

defended—and the tie which bound the states together was of uncertain strength. Our people as a whole were groping in the political twilight more or less confused and only dimly perceived their essential unity. It required the shock of *physical* separation to demonstrate that we were *politically* inseparable, and the dreadful sacrifices of civil war to put beyond dispute the *fact* of nationality.

Prior to the Spanish-American War we vaguely apprehended that we constituted a nation among a family of nations, but we held ourselves aloof from the family concerns except such as affected the members on this side of the Atlantic. From that conflict we emerged a broadened empire with overseas possessions, and a flag carried half around the world. Our comfortable seclusion had gone; our political activities could no longer be confined to the Western Hemisphere. We became a world power; but, because Washington's admonition against "entangling alliances" still dominated our thoughts, we did not perceive that this entailed world responsibilities which, with the coming of the occasion, we should be compelled to assume. That occasion has now come, and these responsibilities we are beginning to face. They will more clearly appear as time passes, and they are not ended with the termination of the war; for it is no longer true, if it ever was true, that European international problems are no concern of ours. For the next few years it is certain they will constitute our chief concern, and they will never hereafter cease to demand our careful consideration and solicitude.

Our entrance as a participant in this war signalized the beginning of a new phase of our national existence, and a new era in our international relations. The extent and character of the changes which will occur cannot be completely foreseen. Much will appear to begin with only in the form of newly acquired tendencies, the practical operation and effect of which will become slowly apparent, but which will be of profound and far-reaching consequence nevertheless. What, for example, will be the character and extent of our future participation in the international policies and politics of Europe? And what will be the effect of such participation upon our own institutions and people? Will there result radical alterations in our trade relations with the countries with whom we are allied, and the countries against whom we have been waging war? What will be the effect upon our policies and laws regulating big business, of the demonstrated inapplicability and inefficiency of these regulations in time of international stress? Has the argument for government ownership been strengthened or weakened by the extended incursions of the national government into the domain of railroad and other business management and control? To the solution of these and other grave problems we must come, with chastened spirit and courageous hearts determined to play our part in the new world with credit and honor. It is no part of my purpose to undertake an extended discussion of the practical side of any of these problems. It must be apparent to every one that the field of national responsibility will be immensely broadened as a result of the war, and there will be presented questions not only relating to this phase of the matter but questions no less important relating to the power of the national government under the Constitution to deal with them. To this question of constitutional power, particularly as it affects our world responsibilities, the succeeding discussions will be mainly directed.

Great changes have occurred in the views of public men since the Constitution was adopted respecting the nature of the government which was instituted and the extent and character of the powers conferred upon it. The differences which have from time to time arisen have in large measure ceased to exist. They are no longer so many nor so serious as they once were, but to some extent they still persist. In the main, these differences have grouped themselves about the two fundamental and opposing theories of government which have divided us from the beginning: one, that the organic unit of our political system is the Union, and the other, that it is the states. The difference between these contending schools of political thought has found expression even in the grammatical form and emphasis of our political language. Under the first theory the *United* States *is*, while under the second, the United *States are* a Nation. The nationalistic conception has constantly grown in favor until it has become the prevailing one, and has even begun to go too far in some particulars in that direction, and to threaten the autonomy of the states, something, the preservation of which is vital to our institutions. Local self-government is a cardinal and very precious article in the American political faith. The many evidences of its lessening hold upon the popular belief are greatly to be regretted. In a country such as ours, of vast area and great population, of diversified industries and greatly varied topography and climate, with here a state devoted to agriculture and there a state devoted to manufacturing, with all sorts of distinguishing characteristics, local state governments with independent and adequate powers are essentials, whose destruction would be a disaster only less grave than the destruction of the Union itself. As the Supreme Court has wisely and accurately said: "The Constitution in all of its provisions looks to an indestructible Union composed of indestructible states." State power and national power are in no wise antagonistic; they are complementary and together support a political structure as nearly perfect as human ingenuity has thus far been able to conceive. The primary concern of the states is with individual and local affairs. The primary concern of the Nation is with the interrelations of the states, and their several peoples, and of the sovereign whole with the world outside. Any unwarranted encroachment upon the former or any captious restriction of the latter must be alike avoided, if the symmetry of the great governmental structure designed by the founders is to be preserved. In the field of constitutional power which it is my purpose to invite you to enter no such conflict can possibly arise because it is a field from which the states are, in any event, absolutely excluded.

In all matters of external sovereignty the powers of the Nation are not only supreme but exclusive, and the question whether a given power in this field shall be exercised by the general government or by the states, can never arise. The question which does arise is startlingly simple and direct: May the power be exercised by governmental agency at all? A negative answer to this question in any given case, it will be seen, might be of the most serious consequence. From this condition of affairs there must result, as will be shown hereafter at length, a rule of constitutional construction radically more liberal than that which obtains in the case of the domestic powers which are distributed between the general government and the states. Any rule of construction which would result in curtailing or preventing action on the part of the national government in the enlarged field of world responsibility which we are entering, might prove highly injurious or embarrassing. We are, for example, vitally concerned in the adoption of every possible safeguard which can be devised to prevent a repetition of the conditions under which Germany came perilously near realizing her dream of European dictatorship. If it should be necessary for us now, or hereafter, to assume burdens strange to our diplomacy in order to secure our future safety, it would be most unfortunate if our government should feel obliged to decline the assumption of such burdens for any real or fancied lack of constitutional power.

It has been seriously suggested that we should take no part in the adjustment of the so-called European questions, but the war being ended we should leave the European belligerents to settle their own affairs in their own way. No suggestion could be more fallacious. The balance of Europe has become a matter with which we are profoundly concerned. One of the grave dangers of this war has been that Germany might become the master of Europe; and it always will be of vital importance to us that no single nation shall ever become the master of Europe, for the happening of such a contingency would make that nation automatically the master of the world.

We are seeking for ourselves none of the usual fruits of conquest—neither territory nor indemnity for the vast military expenses we have incurred. But there are things of great importance which we may justly ask. For one thing, we should seek and obtain in this general world accounting the formal recognition and adoption of the Monroe Doctrine. That would be little to ask of our Allies, and little to exact from our enemies, and it might hereafter prove of incalculable value to us. The Monroe Doctrine is an essential part of our defensive policy, since the subjugation of any of the American Republics by a powerful and aggressive nation would constitute a standing menace to our own future peace. The reality and gravity of such a menace has not been dissipated because autocracy has been driven from its European strongholds. That desirable condition of affairs may not be permanent; but whether it be or not, even democracies are not immune from national ambitions, and the desire for territorial expansion is a matter quite apart from forms of government, as our own history has frequently demonstrated. An imperious republic might be as dangerous and undesirable a neighbor as an imperial monarchy. In any event, the Monroe Doctrine is, and probably always will be, a matter of grave national importance, whose abandonment under an excess of sentiment to the effect that the world had finally and perpetually been made safe for democracy would be supremely unwise. If such a sentiment should turn out to be well founded, no harm will result from the maintenance of this traditional policy, and if, on the other hand, it should unfortunately, but quite possibly, transpire that the sentiment is without foundation, the abandonment of the doctrine might prove expensively and seriously injurious.

Important as this doctrine is, it has, nevertheless, thus far rested upon nothing more substantial than our own assertion. With the exception of Great Britain, it has never received even the tacit approval of Europe. The present situation presents an opportunity which may never come again, to obtain for it the force of international sanction.

The Peace Council about to convene in Europe will be the most important gathering of men ever assembled together. The future worth of human society, the future peace of nations, the future progress and orderly liberty of mankind, are involved in its deliberations. The world has never responded to a summons of greater moment for nobler task. The call which comes to us is to the Nation whose people are one and whose frontiers mark the limits beyond which we dare not be partisans. To this conference, so big with fateful consequences, our Allies will send the wisest and most astute of their statesmen. To meet and counsel with them, to aid in formulating lasting and righteous covenants for the world's welfare, are heavy and solemn responsibilities fit to be borne only by the greatest and most sagacious of our own. That such, and only such, have been selected we shall all fervently hope until they shall have acted, when we shall know.

CHAPTER II

THE POWERS OF THE NATIONAL GOVERNMENT

The form of government under which we live, wisely established by our forefathers, is that of a representative, self-limited democracy, as distinguished, on the one hand, from an absolute or direct democracy and, on the other hand, from an absolute monarchy, either of which is an unsafe foundation upon which to rest the political institutions of a free people. The fault of the former is that it constitutes an impossible attempt to carry on the highly complex and multiplex political activities of modern civilization with the crude methods of primitive society; the vice of the latter is that it completely suppresses the *will*, if not the *wishes* of the governed. The dangerous tendency of the one is toward anarchy, for where everybody rules by direct action, the distinction between government and people disappears, with the result, finally, that there is no government at all, but only a mob, passing spasmodic and temporary resolutions. The sure course of the other is toward despotism, for where an autocrat rules, government ceases to be an appliance to preserve liberty and becomes a weapon to destroy it. Representative government avoids both extremes: the first, by devolving the actual operations of government upon agents selected by the people themselves, who thus have the opportunity to appropriate the services of their most capable members; and the second, by retaining ultimate power in the hands of the people, and delegating to these agents only the duty of *exercising* such portions of the power as may, from time to time, be deemed wise and necessary. Thus the futility of an attempt on the part of the whole people to operate the government— an intricate task requiring singleness of purpose and concentration of effort—and the danger of centralizing irrevocable and absolute power in the hands of a single ruler, are alike avoided.

Under such a system, sovereignty and government are not interchangeable terms to express the same thing; they stand for distinct and separate things. Sovereignty is in the people as a political organism constituting the Nation; government is an instrumentality of the Nation by which the external and internal functions of this organism are maintained and operated. This distinction is of the utmost importance, for it lies at the foundation of all our political institutions. The *Nation* is a political entity with plenary and unlimited power, holding in its possession complete sovereignty; the *government* is an agency exercising this power and sovereignty within the limits of the authority granted to it by the Nation. This authority will be narrow or broad, rigid or elastic, according to the method adopted for interpreting the grant. But whatever the method, whether we confine the authority to the strict words of the grant, or extend it by implication, or find large powers in the nature of the grant itself, or in the character of the government instituted,—in any case, the Nation is the final source of every power, and the government only an instrumentality created and constituted for the purpose of exercising it.

And not only is the Nation the source of the powers exercised by the general government, but it is the ultimate and continuing source of the powers exercised by the state governments as well; for these powers, while entirely removed from the control of the national *government*, may be modified, taken away or redistributed by the *Nation* with the single exception that no state shall be deprived of its equal representation in the Senate, and even this restriction upon the power of constitutional amendment is self-imposed by the Nation.

Two general classes of powers are possessed and exercised under our scheme of government: (1) those which relate to our *internal* affairs and are divided between state and national governments; and (2) those which relate to our *external* affairs and can be exercised by the national government alone. Among the latter, and most important, are the great powers of war and peace, the treaty-making power, the power to acquire and govern new territory, to regulate foreign commerce, and generally to maintain and control our diplomatic and other relations with foreign countries.

Heretofore, these powers have seemed remote and have received relatively scant general consideration. Our attention has been chiefly absorbed by matters exclusively our own. Suddenly, however, we found ourselves in the midst of a struggle involving the fate of humanity, and the era of national isolation was at an end. The powers of the national government over external affairs, all at once, therefore have assumed new and increased importance, in the light of which, a re-examination of their nature and extent is not only pertinent but may, sooner or later, become highly necessary; for it is certain that hereafter, whether desired or desirable, we shall be obliged to occupy a larger place in the affairs of the world, to participate to a far greater degree in world policies and lend substantial and increased assistance toward the solution of world problems. By reason of our participation in the war we have formed alliances and assumed responsibilities which we cannot wholly lay aside now that the war is ended. America and the world outside have been brought into immeasurably closer relations. Inevitably, we shall be called upon to deal, not only with some of the old questions from a different point of view, but with many new questions which the framers of the Constitution foresaw dimly, or foresaw not at all.

In this new and extended relationship, we shall probably be obliged to extend the scope and application of the familiar meanings of the Constitution, and it may be to *find*—though not to *make*—new meanings.

At the threshold of the inquiry, as already indicated, it will be assumed as fundamental that the authority of the general government is derivative, not primary; that all political power originates with the people and ultimately rests there. This, however, does not carry us very far, since the question is not what is the source of the original power, but how much of it may be exercised. From the beginning there has been substantial agreement as to the correctness of the general formula, but wide diversity of opinion as to its application in practice and in detail. At the one extreme, it has been insisted that the general government possesses only such powers as are *expressly* granted by the Constitution strictly construed; and, at the other extreme, it has been claimed, and still is sometimes claimed, that the so-called "general welfare clause" is a grant of practically unlimited power, instead of being, where it is found in the preamble, simply a statement of one of the ends to be accomplished by the exercise of the conferred powers; and instead of being, where it is found in Article 1, Section 8, only a limitation upon the taxing power. The true limit lies somewhere between these two extreme contentions, but the precise point has never received common recognition. Between the view which would put the national government in a straight-jacket of strict construction and that which would set it adrift upon a boundless sea of power, all varieties and shades of opinion are to be found. The governmental powers about which we are inquiring, are not embodied in a compact between parties standing upon opposite sides of a matter, nor in an ordinary act of legislation, but in a Constitution of Government. The compact theory of the Constitution proceeds upon a complete misconception of its true nature, for that instrument does not speak the language of *covenant* but the language of *command*. It does not *record* the *understanding* but *declares* the *will* of those who made it. It is not *agreed upon* but *ordained* and *established*. It is the *result* of agreement among its makers, just as a statute is the *result* of agreement among its makers, but it is not itself an agreement any more than a statute is itself an agreement. It is not a league or confederation or compact among a number of equal and independent states, but a mandate from those who constitute the sovereign source of all political power—state as well as national—declaring their collective will and creating governmental agencies to carry it into effect. The agencies thus constituted, it must be assumed, were designed by their creators to be clothed with full power to accomplish the general objects for which they were brought into existence. To this end, therefore, the Constitution must be broadly construed, so that the design of its makers may not fail of execution.

To ascertain the nature and extent of the powers conferred by this Constitution, the ends for which they were granted must be kept steadily in mind. Having discovered the general purpose of the instrument, its provisions must be construed with reference to that purpose, and so as to subserve it.[1]

The two classes of powers I have described, not only differ widely in their nature, but the result of denying or curtailing the authority of the general government to exercise them in the one case and in the other, is vastly different. The rules of construction, which apply when the government undertakes to deal with *internal* matters, may not apply, in the case of *external* affairs, in the same way, or to the same degree, or, conceivably, in some cases, may not apply at all. In ascertaining the meaning of language, not only must the *words* be considered, but the objects to which these words relate must be taken into account as well. If you say, for example, "I have *control* over my children and my property," you use precisely the same words to describe your relationship to the two objects; but, nevertheless, the power which you connote by these identical words is

[1] 12 Wall. 530.

not the same. The control in the one case carries with it the power to sell your property; it does not, in the other case, enable you to sell your children, because the scope and extent of the power is restricted by paramount rules which forbid your doing so.

Again, for example: the Constitution grants to Congress the "power to regulate commerce with foreign nations and among the several states, etc." The words which confer the power to regulate *foreign* commerce are the same words which confer the power to regulate *interstate* commerce, but the objects to which they apply are different, and hence the power, while the same in terms, may be, and, in fact, is, quite different in scope and extent. The general government in dealing with foreign commerce, acting as the government of a Nation possessing full powers of sovereignty and as the only government capable of acting in that matter at all, may altogether prohibit the exportation to, or importation from, any foreign country of any particular commodity, or of all articles of commerce whatsoever. The exercise of the power to place an embargo upon foreign commerce may be required by considerations of the most vital nature; and it must be assumed that the general government possesses such power under well established principles of international law. But no such degree of power may be exercised over the commercial relations of the several states among themselves, since international law has no application to our internal affairs, and since the prohibition of an interchange of commodities among the states would subvert the plain design of the commerce clause as applied to interstate trade, namely, to secure commerce among the states against conflicting and discriminating state regulations, and to *insure a free interchange of all legitimate commodities among the citizens thereof*.

While holding that regulation of interstate commerce as to certain exceptional articles, such as lottery tickets, diseased cattle, etc., may take the form of prohibition, the Supreme Court of the United States has clearly recognized the distinction just made. In Groves v. Slaughter,[2] after showing that under the power to regulate foreign commerce, Congress passes "embargo and non-intercourse acts," the Court proceeds:

"The power to regulate commerce among the several states is given in the same section and in the same language. But it does not follow that the power may be exercised to the same extent. . .

"The United States are considered as a unit in all regulations of foreign commerce, but this cannot be the case where the regulations are to operate among the several states. The law must be equal and general in its provisions. Congress cannot pass a non-intercourse law, as among the several states; nor impose an embargo that shall affect only a part of them."

And Chief Justice Fuller in The Lottery Cases [3] puts in clear and forcible language the same distinction:

"As in effect before observed, the power to regulate commerce with foreign nations and the power to regulate interstate commerce are to be taken *diverso intuitu*, for the latter was intended to secure equality and freedom in commercial intercourse as between the states, not to permit the creation of impediments to such intercourse; while the former clothed Congress with that power over international commerce, pertaining to a sovereign nation in its intercourse with foreign nations, and subject, generally speaking, to no implied or reserved power in the states. The laws which would be necessary and proper in the one case would not be necessary or proper in the other."

[2] 15 Peters 449, 505.
[3] 188 U. S. 321, 373.

It is true, this language is found in a dissenting opinion, but there is nothing in the majority opinion which conflicts with the general principle announced.

It is equally important to bear in mind this distinction in connection with other powers exercised by the general government over foreign, as distinguished from domestic affairs. The reasons which impelled the framers of the Constitution to enumerate and limit the powers of the general government in its dealings with the several states and with the domestic affairs of the people, had little or no application to external or international affairs. The apprehension of those who favored restricting the powers of the general government, was not so much based on fear of national power as it was on jealousy for state power. Though both sentiments found expression, that which looked to the preservation of the local state authority over internal affairs was the one which was prominently manifested. Neither in the Framers' Convention nor in any of the ratifying conventions was there apparent any opposition to the plan of conferring upon the general government adequate and complete power over external affairs. It seemed to be generally recognized that such power could appropriately be exercised only by that government, and that the states were incompetent to exercise it except in combination. In the distribution of powers, therefore, the general government was not only made the depository of all authority over external matters, but express prohibitions against the exercise of any such authority by the several states were inserted in the Constitution as well. It is certain, therefore, that if power to deal with any specific external question be denied the general government, the authority will not devolve upon the state governments, or any of them, as having been reserved by the Tenth Amendment, since these governments have not only been rendered incompetent by the prohibitions of the Constitution, but, also, because **it** is inherently impossible for the *several* states, acting *separately*, to deal with matters which concern them only in their *combined* capacity as *united* states. The effect of denying power to the general government over any domestic matter is, therefore, wholly different from the effect of a similar denial in the case of external matters. Generally speaking, to the extent that authority in the former case is denied to the general government, it is affirmed to the state governments; but to the extent such authority in the latter case is denied to the general government, its exercise is precluded altogether; and if the power denied be a necessary or useful one, the effect is not to enrich the state, but only to impoverish the Nation. In view of these considerations, every intendment should be indulged in favor of a claim, on the part of the general government, to the possession of complete power—at least, so far as useful or necessary—over external matters. In all our intercourse with foreign governments, and in all our dealings with external affairs, it must be borne in mind that we are dealing *as* "a national government, and the only government in this country which has the character of nationality," [4] and *with* matters that have been completely withdrawn from the state governments. Within our own borders, in our relations among ourselves we have *many* governments exercising carefully *distributed*

[4] 12 Wall. 457, 555.

powers; in our relations with the outside world we have *one* government exercising *undivided* power. "Toward foreign powers the country has no seam in its garment; it exists in absolute unity as a nation and with full and undisputed national resources." [5] "For local interests the several states of the Union exist, but for international purposes, embracing our relations with foreign nations, we are but one people, one nation, one power." [6]

By the Tenth Amendment it is provided: "The powers not delegated to the United States by the Constitution, nor prohibited by it to the states, are reserved to the states respectively, or to the people." The effect of this is to recognize that every political power originally possessed by the people of the United States is disposed of in one of three ways: (1) it is vested in the national government; (2) it is reserved to the states, or (3) it is still held, as undistributed, by the people. In thus parceling out the totality of political power, it must be assumed that the intention was to vest in one government or the other, every power, the exercise of which would contribute to the usefulness of government as an agency to promote the public good, and to withhold only such as, for sound reasons of public policy, ought not to be vested in any government. To assume less than this, is to indulge the absurd supposition that state and national governments were instituted for the purpose of achieving certain great ends, but that the necessity of conferring adequate power of attainment was entirely disregarded. The state governments, as already stated, are confined in

[5] Bancroft, History of the Constitution, 331.
[6] 130 U. S. 606.

their operations to their own boundaries, and from the nature and structure of our governmental system, as well as by the prohibitions of the Constitution, they can exercise no power externally. It follows, then, that the reservation to the respective states can have no reference to any power to be exerted externally, but refers to internal power exclusively, and that every power over external affairs, not vested in the general government, is held in reserve by the people, and, therefore, incapable of practical exercise.

The rule of construction applicable to state constitutions is that the state government may exercise every power appropriate to governmental administration unless prohibited; and that the legislature, being regarded as the primary depository of such power, is to exercise it, unless by the Constitution devolved upon or from its very nature obviously appertaining to some other department of the government. As to all *domestic* matters, except such as are prohibited, there is, therefore, a complete distribution of power: first, to the general government over subjects enumerated, and, second, to the respective state governments over all unenumerated subjects. Nothing in this field essential to government, is left unprovided for by mischance or oversight; the distribution of power is complete; every conceivable contingency may be dealt with by one governmental agency, or the other, unless authority to do so has been *deliberately* withheld.

In external affairs, however, there is no residuary agency; the sole agency capable of acting is the national government. Is it not reasonable to assume that those who were so careful to avoid any lapse or loss of active power in the case of *internal* matters, were equally solicitous in the case of *external* affairs? If this be answered affirmatively, as it must be, did their expression fall short of their meaning? To put the extreme case: If the framers of the Constitution have omitted to specify affirmatively some highly useful and important external power, is it therefore to be withheld by virtue of the doctrine which limits the general government to the powers expressly granted, and such as are auxiliary thereto? Or, on the other hand, does the fact that they were dealing with a class of powers, sufficiently numerous to be difficult of exhaustive enumeration, but which, whether enumerated or not, might, at any time, require *exercise*, and perhaps very *prompt exercise*, and as to which there was no residuary governmental agency to whom, upon a sort of *suum cuique* principle, any power omitted would automatically fall, justify the application of the rule which governs the construction of state constitutions, namely, that the government may exercise all such powers unless prohibited? In other words, does anything *result* to the general government from the fact that in this exclusive field of external sovereignty powers are not distributed but are assembled? A brief reference to some of the incidents preceding and accompanying the framing and adoption of the Constitution, may assist us in determining the proper answer to these interrogatories. Prior to the Revolution the colonies were independent of each other, but all owed common allegiance to Great Britain. They possessed certain powers of internal government, but they had no power whatever to act in any external matter. Their first step looking to a redress of grievances was taken not separately but unitedly. It consisted of bringing together and causing to be organized the Continental Congress, composed, finally, of delegates from each of the thirteen colonies.

As stated by the Supreme Court in Penhallow v. Doane,[7] this Congress was purely a revolutionary body and possessed the supreme and sovereign powers of war and peace, adequate to every national emergency. These powers were limited only by the objects of the Revolution, and to determine what they were, we have only to ascertain what were in fact exercised.[8] The second Congress, among other things, raised an army, provided a currency, created a navy, organized a treasury and post-office, and finally adopted the Declaration of Independence. Nationality was inherent from the beginning. The sovereign Nation and the independent states, conceived at the same time, were born together. By the Declaration of Independence the colonies did not sever their connection with Great Britain as *separate colonies* but as the *United States of America*, and they declared not the *several* but the *united* colonies to be free and independent states—not Massachusetts, not New York, not Virginia, separately, but all combined and united. Together, and not separately, they waged the war; together they made peace; and together they entered the family of nations not as thirteen distinct sovereignties but as *one sovereign Nation*. The several states never exercised the powers of external sovereignty; they were never recognized by any foreign government; they never possessed the attributes of

[7] 3rd Dall. 54, 80.
[8] *Ibid.*

nationality. When the treaty of peace was made with Great Britain and the *Declaration* of Independence became a *fact*, it is impossible to escape the conclusion that all powers of external sovereignty finally passed from the Kingdom of Great Britain to the people of the thirteen colonies as one political unit, and not to the people separately as thirteen political units. This great historical fact, which stands out so clearly now, was not then universally recognized or conceded. State jealousy was a very strong and disturbing factor. It was a time of doubt and confusion, of distrust and suspicion, and the passionate desire of the people for state autonomy prevented a full realization of their status as a nation. But even under the Confederation there were those, not blinded by the prejudice of locality, who saw clearly the essential fact. One such was James Wilson, a signer of the Declaration of Independence, afterwards to become one of the framers of the Constitution and a Justice of the Supreme Court of the United States. Writing upon the question of the challenged power of the Congress of the Confederation to incorporate the Bank of North America, he said:

"The United States have general rights, general powers, and general obligations, not derived from any particular states, nor from all the particular states, taken separately; but resulting from the union of the whole. . .

"To many purposes the United States are to be considered as one undivided, independent nation, and as possessed of all the rights and powers and properties by the law of nations incident to such.

"Whenever an object occurs to the direction of which no particular state is competent, the management of it must of necessity belong to the United States in Congress assembled. There are many objects of this extended nature. . .

"The act of independence was made before the Articles of Confederation. This act declares that 'these *United Colonies*' (not enumerating them separately) 'are free and independent states; and that as free and independent states *they* have full power to do *all* acts and things which independent states may of right do'.

"The confederation was not intended to weaken or abridge the powers and rights to which the United States were previously entitled. It was not intended to transfer any of those powers or rights to the particular states, or any of them. If, therefore, the power now in question was vested in the United States before the confederation, it continues vested in them still. The confederation clothed the United States with many, though perhaps not with sufficient powers; but of none did it disrobe them."

Upon the theory that sovereignty over the country embraced by the colonies passed from the Crown to the whole people as a political unit, it was not an uncommon opinion among the colonists that the unappropriated crown lands vested not in the people of the colonies or states in which these lands were respectively situated, but in the whole people.[9]

At any rate, in recognition of some such doctrine, the unoccupied territory belonging to some of the colonies was ceded to the United States. This, it should be observed, except in the case of Georgia and North Carolina, was under the Articles of Confederation. Nowhere in the Articles of Confederation was the power to acquire or govern territory specifically given to the United States, nor could it be inferred from any power which was given. This territory, then, it would seem, could only be acquired and governed upon the theory that such power *resulted* from the sum of the powers granted, or from the fact of nationality. Whatever

[9] Chisholm *v.* Georgia, 2 Dall. 470.

may be the conclusion otherwise, it seems clear that external sovereignty never was possessed—certainly it never was exercised—by the states severally. The use of the term "states" to describe the constituent members of the Union is itself confusing, since it carries an implication of sovereignty not justified by analysis. A "state" in the international sense means an international sovereignty possessing, as essential attributes, equality in the family of nations and full power to contract with other sovereignties. A state in the American Union possesses neither. Its equality is with reference to sister states, not with reference to international states; and it has no power to contract even with a sister state without obtaining the consent of Congress. Each state of the Union is independent of every other state and *exercises* supreme powers, but its *will* is not supreme since it is subject to the paramount will of the Nation, which, by a vote of three-fourths of its members, may strip the state of any of its powers, and vest them in the general government.

In one of the most notable utterances of the Framers' Convention that has been preserved, Rufus King insisted that the states were not sovereign—at least not in any complete sense: "They did not possess the peculiar features of sovereignty, they could not make war, nor peace, nor alliances, nor treaties. Considering them as political beings, they were dumb, for they could not speak to any foreign sovereignty whatever; they were deaf, for they could not hear any proposition from any such sovereignty; they had not even the organs or faculties of defense or offense, for they could not of themselves raise troops, or equip vessels for war."

And he contended that a union of the states was a union of the men who composed them from whence a *national* character resulted to the whole.[10]

The debates in, and proceedings of, the Framers' Convention, in so far as they were preserved and published, clearly evince that it was the intention of the makers of the Constitution to vest in the national government complete authority over external affairs. The sixth paragraph of the Virginia plan declared that the national legislature "ought to be empowered to enjoy the legislative rights vested in Congress by the Confederation, and *moreover* to legislate in all cases to which the *separate* states are incompetent, etc." [11] This paragraph was adopted and reported to the Committee of the Whole. In the Convention it was debated, and finally amended so as to read "and moreover to legislate in all cases for the general interest of the Union, and also in those to which the states are *separately* incompetent"; and in this form, it was referred to the Committee of Detail for the purpose of reporting a constitution. This Committee had no power except to carry out the will of the Convention, and, as it does not appear that there was any change of opinion, it may be fairly assumed that the Committee and the members of the Convention meant that the Constitution should conform with the resolution, and that in their judgment it did so. In this connection, let us turn for a moment to the preamble. It declares that the objects of the Constitution are "to form a more perfect union, establish justice, insure domestic tranquillity, provide for the common

[10] Madison Papers, 5 Elliott's Debates, 212–213.
[11] Madison Papers, 5 Elliott, 127.

defense, promote the general welfare and secure the blessings of liberty to ourselves and our posterity." This is not an enumeration of *substantive powers*, but is an enumeration of the great and comprehensive *ends*, for the accomplishment of which the Constitution was ordained and established. The substantive powers conferred upon the national government, as well as those reserved to the states, are the means to these ends; but it is the ends which are essential; the means are only important in so far as they contribute to the ends. Hence the wisdom of the rule already referred to, that the Constitution must be construed with reference to these ends and so as to subserve them. So far as they may be subserved by the regulation or control of domestic affairs, the state governments may generally act in those cases where the general government is not empowered to act; but whenever the regulation or control of external affairs is necessary, the ends must be realized by the activities of the national government, or, practically speaking, not at all, for he who drives must be given the lines; and a power reserved to a hundred million drivers is in effect a power which does not exist, since it cannot be translated into action until transferred to the government by the long, tedious and almost impossible process of Constitutional amendment.

We are now ready, I think, for the conclusion which these premises justify. The men who made the Constitution were deeply learned in the science of government. They intended to confer complete and adequate power over domestic affairs to the extent that governmental action was appropriate and necessary or useful.

They did not intend to provide less completely in the case of external affairs. In all matters of *internal* sovereignty, when the Constitution was framed, the original reservoir of power was in the states; portions therefrom were delegated to the national government; the residue was retained by the states. It is to this class of powers that the language of the Supreme Court in Ex Parte Virginia,[12] appropriately applies: "Every addition of power to the general government involves a corresponding diminution of the governmental powers of the states. *It is carved out of them.*" And it must have been only this class of powers which Chief Justice Waite had in mind when, in delivering the opinion of the Court in Munn v. Illinois,[13] he said:

"When the people of the United Colonies separated from Great Britain, they changed the form, but not the substance, of their government. They retained for the purposes of government all the powers of the British Parliament and, through their State Constitutions, or other forms of social compact, undertook to give practical effect to such as they deemed necessary for the common good and the security of life and property. All the powers which they retained they committed to their respective states, unless in express terms or by implication reserved to themselves. Subsequently, when it was found necessary to establish a National government for national purposes, a part of the powers of the states and of the people of the states was granted to the United States and the people of the United States. This grant operated as a further limitation upon the powers of the states, so that now the governments of the states possess all the powers of the Parliament of England, except such as have been delegated to the United States or reserved by the people. The reservations by the people are shown in the prohibitions of the constitutions."

[12] 100 U. S. 339.
[13] 94 U. S. 113.

With reference to the powers of *internal* sovereignty, therefore, it is quite logical to conclude that the authority of the national government should be limited *to* the *grants* of the Constitution, leaving the residue to the states, to be exercised by their respective governments, except as limited *by* the *prohibitions* of the state or National constitutions. Since these powers, so far as they are vested in the general government, have been "carved out of" the mass of state governmental powers, it would seem to follow, indubitably, that those not appearing by express words or natural implication to have been severed from the mass still remain in their original place. Not so, however, with respect to the powers of external sovereignty. These were never possessed by the states, or the people of the states separately, and, hence, could not have been delegated, since the states or the people of the states could not delegate something they did not have. These powers passed directly to the Nation as the result of successful revolution. They were never exercised, they were never possessed, by any government except the government which, for the time being, represented the Nation. When the Constitution was framed, therefore, the undivided powers of *external* sovereignty were in the Union, which antedated the Constitution and was made "more perfect" by it. Hence, the disposition of these powers did not involve taking something from the mass of state power—did not involve an apportionment between the states and the Nation—for they already belonged to the Nation, and the only question to be determined was, What shall be given to the general government, and made active, and what shall be reserved to the people, and lie dormant?

This brings us to the point where it would seem to be clear that, with respect to the powers of *external* sovereignty, the general government occupies a relation to the national Constitution not unlike that which the state governments occupy toward their respective constitutions, namely, that of sole governmental administrator; and, inasmuch as the powers of government must be commensurate with the ends for which the government was instituted in order to insure attainment, a presumption arises that every necessary power is conferred unless prohibited.

The question may be viewed from a slightly different angle. The framers of the Constitution were familiar with the principles governing the intercourse of nations. They knew that the provisions of the Constitution could have no extra-territorial force, but that the extra-territorial operations of the United States must be governed by the law of nations. They knew that under this law, all nations, however constituted, were co-equal, and that the highest duty of every nation was that of self-preservation.

As early as 1758, Vattel had written: "Whatever is lawful for one nation is lawful for another; and whatever is unjustifiable in the one is equally so in the other." With this understanding, the United States was introduced into the family of nations, to be governed by the law of nations, equal in power and in right to every other nation, and possessing, as its highest right and most imperious duty, the right and duty of self-preservation. And with this understanding, the government was

created and constituted as the sole agency of the Nation
in all its external relations, charged with the responsibility of preserving it and of maintaining its equality.
For the accomplishment of these ends, it must be assumed, as a necessary and self-evident postulate, that
no legitimate power would be intentionally withheld.
It is axiomatic that a general agent has power to do
anything, not specifically excepted, which falls within
the scope of his general authority. The principle is not
without application to the national government when
dealing with external affairs, where it is not only a general agent but an exclusive agent.

As a conclusion from all that has been said, the rule
of construction may well be formulated thus: Where the
powers claimed for the general government are to be
subtracted from the mass of original state powers, that
is, where they relate to domestic and internal affairs,
the claim must be justified by the express grants of the
Constitution, or by the implications arising therefrom;
but where the powers claimed are among those originally
acquired and always exclusively held by the Nation,
that is, where they relate to external affairs, the claim
is justified unless the powers are prohibited by the
Constitution, or unless contrary to the fundamental
principles upon which it was established. In that view
of the question "the reservations by the people are shown
in the prohibitions of the Constitution," and in the restrictive implications involved in these fundamental
principles.

What is the basis of the rule of construction applicable
to a state constitution, by which the government constituted by it is limited not *to* the things granted but *by*

the things prohibited? I do not remember to have ever seen it stated, but obviously it must be this: that the exigencies of governmental administration, because of their great variety and constant augmentation, cannot be foreseen and consequently cannot be enumerated; and it is better to risk an occasional abuse of power (which is, after all, under our system of representative responsibility, very slight) than it is to incur the inconveniences and dangers arising from lack of effective power. In all matters of external sovereignty these reasons apply with equal force to the general government.

The result does not flow from a claim of inherent power, but from the application of a legitimate and logical rule of construction. The sovereign will of the Nation is embodied in the Constitution and its exercise by the government is measured thereby; but in the one case it is manifested by what that instrument affirms and in the other case by what it fails to negative. Thus, for example, the power to make such international agreements as do not constitute treaties in the constitutional sense, the power to acquire territory by discovery and occupation, the power to expel undesirable aliens, none of which are affirmed, nevertheless exist under and by warrant of the Constitution so construed.

CHAPTER III

THE EXTERNAL POWERS—EXTENT AND LIMITATIONS

It is time we realized not in phrases merely but in fact, that the Constitution is not a petrification, nor the charter of a petrification. This is a progressive Nation in a progressive world. As the Nation goes forward the government, which has been organized to put the will of the Nation into operation, must go forward with it and in aid of it; but if the activities of the government are too strictly limited, a drag upon, instead of an aid to this forward progress will result. This does not mean that the powers of the government are not fixed, but it does mean that they are not fixed within any narrow or rigid bounds. It has been frequently said that the meaning of the Constitution does not change, and this is true; but the things which fall within the scope of the Constitution constantly change. As these changes come—very profound in their character sometimes—the old powers are sufficiently comprehensive to embrace them. It is not necessary to create new powers to meet the altered conditions any more than it is necessary to coin new words to describe them; the old powers and the old words possess an inherent elasticity which gives them an indefinite capacity for new extensions and applications. The Nation is not an ingeniously constructed mechanism made to go, as a clock goes, without inward capacity; it is an organism having inherent power to be and to grow in response to the indwelling forces which make it an organism. As it grows, the Constitution which clothes its government with power must grow also lest it be left naked and defenseless at some vulnerable point. The Constitution was not made alone for those who framed it and adopted it. It was made for us who followed them, and for those who will follow us in the centuries yet to come. As it served for the small affairs of the fathers it serves for the large affairs of their sons, and will serve for the vast affairs of unborn generations; not because its meaning changes but because its capacity for adaptation is indefinitely flexible. The progress of every sort—social, political, financial, mechanical and economic—which has been made since the Constitution was written has been so vast in extent and so revolutionary in character, that an entirely new world has resulted. However little the specific changes were foreseen, this new world was within the contemplation of those who adopted the Constitution, and that instrument applies if the new conditions fall within its scope, not for the reason that those who framed and those who adopted the Constitution *intended* it to apply to these specific conditions—for they could not have intended something of which they were completely ignorant—but because, at least, there is nothing in their words to justify the assumption that if the specific conditions had been foreseen they would have been in terms excepted from the operations of the general government. When, for example, provision was made for congressional regulation of commerce the thing chiefly in mind was transportation by water. Land transportation was limited and primitive, and governmental regulation, either infra-state or inter-state, was exceedingly simple. The application of steam; the weaving together of the states by a network of steel highways, upon which moves a commerce vastly greater than all the commerce of the world in 1787; the invention of the telegraph, the telephone, wireless telegraphy; the advent and development of aërial navigation—all these were beyond the thoughts of the fathers in their most exalted visions; but the commerce clause includes them as completely as it originally included the stage coach, and as it will include all future means of commercial intercourse and transportation, however strange to the experience of that older day and of this newer day they may be. Without this capacity for indefinite extension the written Constitution long since would have become a tradition, and the Union itself, perhaps, have fallen apart from its own weakness. Fortunately, the doctrine of strict construction which denied this capacity did not prevail, but was decisively overthrown *in limine*, since when the rule has undergone a process of gradual but continual and certain liberalization.

The earlier decisions of the Supreme Court laid down the doctrine of the implied powers, namely, that Congress was not only vested with the expressly enumerated powers of the Constitution but also possessed implied power to enact any legislation necessary and proper to carry into effect all powers vested by the Constitution, and that, in exercising this implied power, Congress possessed a range of choice so wide as to be practically unlimited.

But as the Nation grew and novel conditions developed, governmental problems arose which could not be

solved by reference to any of the granted powers or by
recourse to the implications arising therefrom, and legislation was enacted and upheld by the Court if the
authority could be deduced from any grouping of the
express powers, or from the sum of them all. The
process did not end here. From time to time Congress
enacted legislation which could not be justified under
any express power, or any combination of the express
powers, or under all of them combined, nor by virtue of
any reasonable implication capable of being drawn
therefrom. Some of these acts were of a purely administrative character, and have never given rise to a case or
proceeding, so that the judicial power might be invoked;
but others presenting justiceable questions have been
considered by the Supreme Court and their validity sustained. It is not easy to reconcile the conclusions
arrived at in some of these decisions with the sweeping
general statements which have been made, from time
to time, by members of the Court, to the effect that the
national government is one of enumerated powers, and
may exercise *no* power not expressly granted or necessarily implied; although it does not appear that the
rule has been thus stated in any case which involved the
authority of the general government to act in external
affairs.

Congress more than once has passed, and the Supreme
Court has upheld, legislation which could be justified
only upon the hypothesis that there was, under some
conditions, a broader basis for the exercise of power than
that afforded by this conception of the rule; legislation
which must find its support in a rule as broad as that
formulated by Alexander Hamilton: "There are express

and implied powers, and the latter are as effectually delegated as the former; there is also another class of powers which may be called *resulting* powers—resulting from the whole mass of the power of government, and *from the nature of political society*, rather than as a consequence of any especially enumerated power."

The most striking illustration of the application of this broader rule is that involved in the acquisition, and somewhat less clearly, in the government of new territory. There is no provision in the Constitution by which the national government is specifically authorized to acquire territory; and only by a great effort of the imagination can the substantive power to do so be found in the terms of any or all of the enumerated powers. The question arose very early in our history in connection with the Louisiana purchase. It has been asserted that Mr. Jefferson thought the acquisition without constitutional warrant; but what he challenged was not the power to acquire and govern Louisiana but the power to incorporate it into the Union. In the opinion of the Secretary of the Treasury, Albert Gallitan, a statesman of ability and a lawyer of great learning, the acquisition was justified either under the constitutional power to make treaties, or as an exercise of the *inherent right of the United States as a Nation*. Chief Justice Marshall upheld the validity of the acquisition under the treaty-making power, saying that the "government possesses the power of acquiring territory either by conquest or by treaty." [1] The broader basis stated by Mr. Gallatin was neither affirmed nor denied. Mr. Justice Story, in his work on the Constitution, upholds

[1] 1 Peters 542.

the power of the government, but thinks it is not dependent "upon any specific grant" but "flows as an incidental power from its sovereignty over war and treaties." [2]

We have acquired much territory under treaty provisions and by conquest, and in such case the acquisition may be regarded as incidental to the powers mentioned; but we have also acquired territory by original discovery and appropriation alone. Such is the fact with reference to a large portion of Oregon; and such is peculiarly the fact with reference to certain small islands of the sea—the so-called Guano Islands. An act of Congress provides for the acquisition by Executive proclamation of any islands valuable for their deposits of guano, discovered by citizens of the United States and not, at the time of discovery, occupied or possessed by any other government or its citizens. By virtue of the provisions of this act and certain general statutes, offenses committed on these islands are made cognizable in the judicial district "where the offender is found, or into which he is first brought." Some years ago a man named Henry Jones committed a homicide on one of these islands, and having been first brought to the District of Maryland, was there indicted, tried for and convicted of murder. The power of the general government to acquire territory for the United States by simple discovery and occupation was therefore directly involved. The question could not be determined by reference to the war powers or the treaty-making power: there was no war; there was no treaty; there was no one against whom war could be waged; and there was no one with whom a

[2] Story, Constitution, Section 1287.

treaty could be made. Nevertheless, the Supreme Court upheld the validity of the acquisition under the act of Congress, not by virtue of any *constitutional power* but wholly by virtue of the *established principles of international law*. The opinion was rendered by Mr. Justice Gray, who said:

"By the law of nations, recognized by all civilized states, dominion of new territory may be acquired by discovery and occupation, as well as by cession or conquest; and when citizens or subjects of one nation, in its name, and by its authority or with its assent, take and hold actual, continuous and useful possession (although only for the purpose of carrying on a particular business, such as catching and curing fish, or working mines) of territory unoccupied by any other government or its citizens, the nation to which they belong may exercise such jurisdiction and for such period as it sees fit over territory so acquired. This principle affords ample warrant for the legislation of Congress concerning guano islands."

Previous acquisitions of territory had been vindicated as having been made in the exercise of certain specifically granted powers of the Constitution, and as purely incident thereto. In this instance, however, the islands were acquired not as incident to the exercise of some other and distinct power but substantively and under circumstances wholly disconnected from any act save the acquisition itself. We must infer there was no provision, or combination of provisions, from which, in the opinion of the Court, the authority could be derived, since none is mentioned; and we are forced to conclude that the Supreme Court has, in this case, recognized the possession of a power by the General government, not referable to the *terms* of the Constitution—a power, the exercise of which must be regarded as simple usurpation, unless it be conceded that it *resulted* from the whole mass of governmental power, or from the nature of political society, that is, as a necessary consequence of nationality. The act of Congress was upheld not as an exercise of any *constitutionally delegated* power but upon the sole ground that the "dominion of new territory may be acquired by discovery and occupation, as well as by cession or conquest" under a universally recognized principle of international law; and it is this *principle*, and not any *grant or implication* of the Constitution, which, in the unanimous opinion of the Supreme Court, "affords ample warrant for the legislation." No member of that Court has ever repudiated the doctrine thus asserted. It has been followed in subsequent cases without qualification or comment, the Court merely affirming, upon the authority of prior decisions, the power of the general government to acquire territory by discovery and occupation alone, saying that any discussion of the source of its power was unnecessary. It is not easy, therefore, to avoid the conclusion that legislation may be in a sense *extra*-constitutional without being *un*-constitutional. At any rate those who would deny the existence of any governmental power resulting from the fact that the general government alone exercises the attributes of nationality, and is the only government competent to exercise the powers of external sovereignty, must first reject the established doctrine of this case and repudiate our occupation of Oregon and the Guano Islands as being without right or title; for this case constitutes not an exception which proves the general rule but an illustration which destroys it, since the rule for which they contend is that the national government possesses *no* power not delegated by, or necessarily implied from the *words* of the Constitution.

The principle involved in the Jones case is recognized and asserted in other decisions of the Supreme Court. No comprehensive review of these decisions can, of course, be attempted, but a brief reference to some of them may prove instructive. In the Legal Tender Cases,[3] Mr. Justice Strong, speaking for the majority of the court, said that the adoption of the first ten amendments indicated that in the judgment of those who adopted the Constitution there were powers created by it not specified nor deducible from, or ancillary to, any one specified power "but which grew out of the aggregate of powers conferred upon the government, *or out of the sovereignty instituted.*"

Mr. Justice Bradley in a concurring opinion characterized the United States as "a national government and the only government in this country having the character of nationality," and added:

"Such being the character of the General government, it seems to be a self-evident proposition that it is invested with all those inherent and implied powers which, at the time of adopting the Constitution, were generally considered to belong to every government as such, and as being essential to the exercise of its functions."

Early in the history of the country Congress passed the so-called Alien and Sedition Laws, the constitutionality of which was savagely attacked, as well as stoutly defended. The power of the general government to expel undesirable aliens was denied by the Virginia and Kentucky resolutions and upheld by Massachusetts and other northern states. The Alien Act was, by its terms,

[3] 12 Wall. 457.

limited to a period of two years, and never came before the Supreme Court for consideration. The Chinese Exclusion and Expulsion Acts—the latter presenting precisely the same question as that involved in the Alien Act passed almost a century later—were, however, sustained by that Court after full consideration. The Exclusion Act was upheld by virtue of the "accepted maxim of international law that every sovereign nation has the power, as inherent in sovereignty, and essential to self-preservation, to forbid the entrance of foreigners within its dominions, or to admit them only in such cases and upon such conditions as it may see fit to prescribe." [4] The validity of the Expulsion Act was affirmed as a legitimate exercise of the powers of sovereignty as recognized by the law of nations: "the right to exclude or expel all aliens, or any class of aliens, absolutely or upon certain conditions, in war or in peace, being an inherent and inalienable right of every sovereign and independent nation, essential to its safety, its independence and its welfare." [5]

In the last-named case, three justices dissented. The dissenting opinions of Justices Brewer and Field conceded the power of *exclusion* but denied the power of *expulsion*, the former Justice placing the distinction upon the ground that the Constitution having no extraterritorial effect, those who have not come lawfully within our territory cannot claim the protection of its provisions, and, further, that the national government having full control of all matters relating to other nations may have the power to absolutely forbid aliens to

[4] 142 U. S. 659.
[5] 149 U. S. 698.

enter; but that the Constitution has potency everywhere within the limits of our territory, and the powers which the national government may exercise *within that territory* are only such as are conferred by that instrument which nowhere gives the power to remove resident aliens.   These cases and the various opinions, taken together, afford persuasive ground for the contention that powers to be exercised externally are not exclusively derived from, and are, consequently, not limited to, the grants and implications of the Constitution, but may find their warrant outside the terms of that instrument in the accepted rules of international law.   The fact, also, that all such powers are denied the several states lends additional strength to this conclusion.   Indeed, the view of one of the most scholarly and deeply learned jurists the country has ever known, Judge Campbell, a former justice of the Supreme Court of Michigan, seems to be that this circumstance alone may constitute a sufficient basis for the conclusion. He says:

"Under the Constitution of the United States all possible powers must be found in the Union or the states, or else they remain among those reserved rights which the people have retained *as not essential to be vested in any government.*   That which is forbidden to the states is not necessarily in the Union, because it may be among the reserved powers.   *But if that which is essential to government is prohibited to one it must of necessity be found in the other, and the prohibition in such case on the one side is equivalent to a grant on the other.*"

That the general government possesses complete powers of sovereignty over, as well as full ownership in, new territory, is well settled.   The power to acquire new territory being conceded or established, the power

to govern would seem to follow as a necessary consequence. The precise basis upon which it rests, however,
may be important as reflecting light upon the general
question under consideration, as well as suggesting the
scope and extent of the power itself. The property
clause of the Constitution has frequently been quoted
as conferring the power to govern. That clause reads
as follows: "The Congress shall have power to dispose
of, and make all needful rules and regulations respecting
the territory and other property belonging to the
United States." It is, of course, with the utmost defer-
ence to the opinions of the Supreme Court deducing the
power from this provision, that I venture to suggest a
doubt respecting the soundness of the conclusion. Let
us examine the language of the provision. The power
is (1) *"To dispose of . . .* the territory or other property belonging to the United States." It will scarcely
admit of question that here the power or disposal relates
to territory as *property* and not to territory as an *organic
field of government.* The power is (2) *"To make all needful rules and regulations* respecting the territory or other
property belonging to the United States." Here, it is
to be observed, the power is not to *govern* or to make
laws but to make *rules and regulations;* and while it is
true that Congress can make rules and regulations only
by legislating, the words are not such as we should
expect the framers of the Constitution to employ, if
general powers of government had been intended. The
Constitution, as we know, was framed with great care,
and its language chosen with a view to precise expression. In the provision relating to the seat of government (afterwards to be established as the District of

Columbia) and to the places purchased for forts, arse-
nals, and so on, the power prescribed is "to exercise
exclusive legislation in all cases whatsoever over such
district, etc." The exercise of complete governmental
authority is by these words obviously contemplated.
If like power had been intended by the property clause
it is difficult to understand why similar language was
not used instead of words whose ordinary signification
must be strained in order to import the extended meaning attributed to them. There is, moreover, a rule of
legal interpretation—which, unlike some of the laws
that call for its application, accords with common sense
as well—known as the rule of associated words, which
means that a word, like an individual, may be known
by the company it keeps. If a law, for example, forbid
the doing of something in a theater, church, or other
public place, the words "other public place" are not to
be construed as including parks, streets, or open places
but must be confined to places similar to those enumerated, that is, to other *enclosed* public places. On the
other hand, if the law forbid the doing of something in
a park, or street, or other public place, the words "other
public place" in that association of words, are to be
given an exactly opposite construction, that is, they
must be held not to include public buildings but only
other *open* places.

Here the associated words are "territory or other
property." The word *territory* is, therefore, found in
association with the word *property*, and, if susceptible of
a double meaning—that is, of a restricted and also of a
more general meaning—as it is, should be assimilated
to the meaning of the word which it accompanies. The

employment of the word "other" to qualify the word "property" would seem, obviously, to imply that the antecedent "territory" was used in the same sense—that is, in the sense of property—otherwise the word property would mean *simply* property but not *other* property. It must follow, then, that the word *territory* is to be given its proprietary, rather than its political meaning, that is, it is to be interpreted as though the expression had been "lands" or "public domain." That territory as property, and not organic territory, was intended, is also borne out by the consideration that the evident purpose is to include "territory or other property," *wherever situated*, since the only qualification is that it must be something "belonging to the United States." Vast areas of public lands lying within the limits of western states today, constitute "territory . . . belonging to the United States", but toward such lands the relation of the United States is uniformly held to be that of proprietor and not that of sovereign.

Prior to the admission of these states into the Union, Congress occupied toward these lands a double relationship, namely, that of proprietor and that of sovereign. As proprietor it disposed of the lands under the property clause of the Constitution; as sovereign it governed the territory embracing both public lands and private lands. When the territory became a state, the powers of internal sovereignty of the general government passed to the state, but its proprietorship still continued. Under the constitutional grant of power contained in the property clause, Congress might still make rules and regulations of a proprietary character, respecting its territory lying within the limits of the state, but could not legislate with respect to municipal or other purposes, except as the power to do so is recognized by provisions of the Constitution, entirely apart from this particular clause. Since, therefore, the clause under consideration applies to public lands lying within the borders of a state, as well as to those outside, and since the powers of general legislation may not be exercised over such lands within a state, it seems logical to conclude that the power conferred upon Congress was intended to be of that limited character, which may be exercised over all territory or other property of the United States irrespective of locality.

That the usual powers of legislation were not contemplated is indicated from another point of view. It is well established that legislative power cannot be delegated; yet Congress and the courts have again and again recognized the validity of regulations made by groups of miners, or imposed by state or territorial laws, affecting the possession and acquisition of mineral lands constituting part of the public domain.

Mr. Justice Brewer, speaking of such regulations and upholding their binding quality [6] said that Congressional legislation providing for the disposal of public lands savored somewhat of mere rules prescribed by an owner of property; that it was not legislation in the highest sense of that term; and that, as the principal agent of an owner may employ subordinates with limited discretion, Congress may intrust to local legislatures the determination of minor matters respecting the disposal of public lands.

[6] 196 U. S. 126.

Again: the powers described are to be exercised with reference to territory or other property "belonging to" the United States. These are words commonly, though not always, used to denote ownership rather than jurisdiction. To speak of a thing as "belonging to" any one is another way of asserting his proprietorship. That the words were used in this sense when applied to "property" would seem clear, and in this sense they appropriately apply to the word "territory" treated as property. If the framers of the Constitution had intended by this clause to confer both governmental and proprietary powers upon Congress, we should naturally look for language clearly giving the power to deal with territory, not only as property belonging to the United States, but as country subject to the jurisdiction thereof as well.

That an organized subdivision of the outlying national domain is called a territory and that the same term is used in the clause under consideration is a coincidence without substantial significance. It happened to be so designated instead of being called a colony or a province, which in fact it is; but the distinction is nevertheless perfectly clear between *a* territory and *the* territory of the United States. The former is a governmental subdivision—a corporate institution; the latter is merely a portion of the earth's surface—a piece of real estate. It is in the latter sense and not in the former sense that the word is used in this clause of the Constitution; and it is in the latter sense and not in the former sense that the power to make rules and regulations respecting the territory as well as the other property of the United States is conferred.

From these various considerations it would seem to follow that the clause in question is a mere property clause, having no relation to the high powers of general legislation or the sovereign functions of government; and that the authority to *govern* territory of the United States does not come within the intendment of its framers nor flow from its words.

Nevertheless, the power unquestionably exists, although the sources must be traced to considerations quite apart from the property clause of the Constitution. It is a power which no state government can exercise and yet one whose exercise is so palpably essential, that it cannot be supposed to be among the powers impounded by being reserved to the people. It must, therefore, as a matter of imperious necessity, be found among the powers of the general government; and the basis upon which it rests is that of national supremacy. The power to govern, like the power to acquire, new territory is an attribute of sovereignty under the law of nations; and its practical exercise must necessarily attach to the national government as the only agency capable of exercising it. And this brings us to the conclusion that the power to govern, whether regarded as corollary to, or independent of, the power to acquire territory, exists in the national government, not by virtue of an affirmative grant of the Constitution but by virtue of the "ownership of the country in which the territories are, and the right of exclusive sovereignty which must exist in the national government, and can be found nowhere else." [7]

[7] U. S. *vs.* Kagama, 118 U. S. 380.

In 1899, Elihu Root, then Secretary of War, had occasion to formulate the general principles applicable to the government of our over-seas possessions acquired under the treaty of Paris. After saying that the acquisition was the exercise of a power which belonged to us because we were a Nation, and that we possessed all the powers in respect of the acquired territory, and its inhabitants, which any nation in the world has in respect of territory which it has acquired, and that these powers were not subject to any legal limitations except those to be found in the treaty, he added:

"The people of the ceded islands have acquired a moral right to be treated by the United States in accordance with the underlying principles of justice and freedom, which we have declared in our Constitution, and which are the essential safeguards of every individual against the powers of government, not because those provisions were enacted for them but because they are essential limitations inherent in the very existence of the American government." [8]

In legislating for the government of a territory, Congress is not limited to the powers enumerated in the Constitution. Its authority is plenary and subject only to such prohibitions and restrictions as are intended to preclude the action of the legislative department under all circumstances and conditions. Congress, for example, is without power to enact for a territory an *ex post facto* law, or a bill of attainder, since the prohibition against such legislation is absolute and applies irrespective of time or place. The authority of Congress, however, except as thus limited, extends to every form of legislative activity. Its powers are as

[8] Military and Colonial Policy, 161–162.

ample as those of the English Parliament in dealing with the outlying possessions of the British Empire. It possesses and exercises, to use the language of the Supreme Court in National Bank *vs.* Yankton,[9] "all the powers of the People of the United States except such as have been expressly or by implication reserved in the prohibitions of the Constitution."

Whether the Constitution of its own force extends to the territories is a question which has given rise to earnest, and sometimes bitter, differences of opinion. Prior to the Civil War, it was a question of the greatest moment and gravity involving, as it did, the issue as to whether the institution of slavery went to these possessions under the shelter of the Constitution. That question divided the people of the United States into three hostile political camps. The Breckenridge Democrats asserted, in effect, that neither national nor territorial legislation was competent to destroy or impair the title of the slaveholder to his peculiar property; the Republican Party denounced the dogma that the Constitution, of its own force, carried slavery into the territories as a dangerous political heresy, at variance with the provisions of that instrument itself, as well as legislative and judicial precedent; the Douglas Democrats straddled the question by simply announcing their willingness to abide by the decision of the Supreme Court; while Douglas himself declared his adherence to the doctrine that the inhabitants of the territories possessed the inherent right to determine the question for themselves, a doctrine which passed into the political nomenclature of the day, under the name of "squat-

[9] 101 U. S. 133.

ter sovereignty." These contentions are no longer of any direct concern, but they constitute interesting records of the wanderings and gropings of a bygone generation in their search for the true path of constitutional construction, a process which has played a far more important rôle in the development of constitutional government than the people of today, secure in the stability of their institutions, are in the habit of remembering. Indeed, the interpretation of the Constitution and the determination of the scope and extent of the national authority have been influenced by events quite as much as they have been by logic. The framers builded better than they knew; better than any succeeding generation has known. The Nation did not immediately comprehend its own political nature, or at once grasp the extent of its own great powers. It has not reached full realization even now, after the lapse of more than a century of time. We have gradually arrived at an understanding, and are gradually reaching additional understanding of our powers and duties under the Constitution, not by the conscious processes of analysis so much as by exploration and discovery under the compelling pressure of necessity.

The doctrine that the Constitution went of itself into the territories, or into the territory, of the United States, always discredited, has been long since finally and conclusively overthrown; but it does not follow that the inhabitants of these possessions are not entitled to the benefit of the principles embodied in that instrument. The Constitution may be considered from three several points of view—or rather as having been intended to accomplish three distinct general objects. The first of these objects is the *establishment of a system of government;* the second is the *institution of certain controlling political postulates,* to which the operations of government must conform; and the third is the *fixation of certain well settled rights of a fundamental personal character,* intended to safeguard the liberties of the individual against the operations of government itself. The first and second of these objects concern only the United States as a political society. The territories are possessions of this society but are not constituent parts of it; and it is obvious that the provisions of the Constitution relating to these objects have no application to the territories, since their inhabitants can have nothing to do with the selection of President, or members of Congress, or with the organization or operations of the National government or any of its departments. The inhabitants of the territories have, therefore, no *political* rights under the Constitution, but only such as Congress may choose to give them. As to the third and remaining class of provisions, the status of the territories is not so clear. Some of the enumerated rights are of such a character that under our system of government they could not be denied to the inhabitants of a territory or of our possessions any more than they could be taken away from the people of a state. The Supreme Court has suggested that the line of separation lies between certain natural rights enforced in the Constitution by prohibitions against any interference with them, and what may be called artificial or remedial rights peculiar to our system of jurisprudence. Among the former there is included the rights of religious liberty, freedom of speech and of the press, the right to due process of law, the immunities from unreasonable searches and seizures, and against cruel and unusual punishments, and such other immunities as are indispensable to free government. Among the latter class are the rights to citizenship, to suffrage, and to particular methods of procedure.[10]

So it has been suggested that there may be inherent or unexpressed principles which are the basis of all free government which likewise restrain the power of Congress in dealing with the territories and possessions.[11] Except as so limited, then, it may be regarded as settled doctrine that Congress, in legislating for the territories, or national possessions, possesses complete dominion and sovereignty and exercises the combined powers of the general and of a state government; and these limitations upon the powers of Congress, as Mr. Justice Bradley has said, "exist rather by inference and the general spirit of the Constitution . . . than by any express and direct application of its provisions." In other words, such of these individual and civil rights as are beyond the interfering power of Congress, are guaranteed by the fundamental principles of free government rather than by the direct force of the Constitution in which they are formulated. They cannot be denied to the inhabitants of any territory subject to the control of the United States, because they are inherently inviolable; and the Constitution is resorted to not as supreme law for their enforcement but as high proof of their existence and incontrovertible nature.

[10] Downes *vs*. Bidwell, 182 U. S. 271.
[11] *Ibid.*, 290.

CHAPTER IV

THE WAR POWERS—NATURE, BASIS AND DISTRIBUTION

Thus far we have been discussing those external powers of the national government which appear to exist independently of the specific grants of the Constitution. The conclusions to which we have come, however, are not without relevance in the consideration now to be given certain other external powers which are expressly enumerated. These powers, whether enumerated or unenumerated, are alike in being characterized by the fact that they are beyond the competence of the several states, and to the extent they do not find the full measure of their exercise in the authority of the general government, must remain dormant; and in the fact that, unlike the internal or domestic powers, they are to be exercised and interpreted in the light of that body of rules which regulates the intercourse of nations. It may be said further, that if it be true that, without reference to the affirmative grants of the Constitution, complete authority exists in the general government to deal adequately with all external affairs, unless and except as prohibited by the Constitution or contrary to fundamental principle, it follows, *a fortiori*, that the exercise of expressly enumerated powers of like character is not to be restricted, by any rule of interpretation, within narrower limits.

It may be noted in passing that the very power to *wage* war is not expressly written into the Constitution though it is, of course, necessarily implicit in that group of powers, which are expressly granted, known as the war powers. These powers are divided between Congress and the President, and, briefly stated, are as follows:

1. Congress is given power to declare war, grant letters of marque and reprisal, make rules concerning captures on land and water, raise and support armies, provide and maintain a navy, make rules for the government and regulation of the land and naval forces; to provide for calling forth the militia to execute the laws of the Union, suppress insurrections, and repel invasions; to provide for organizing, arming, and disciplining the militia, and for governing such part of them as may be employed in the service of the United States, reserving to the states the appointment of officers, and the authority of training the militia, according to the discipline prescribed by Congress.

2. The President is designated as the Commander-in-Chief of the Army and Navy of the United States, and of the militia of the several states when called into the actual service of the United States.

If what has already been said generally, respecting the self-existent character of the external powers of the national government, be granted, the power to declare and the power to wage war, together with all other subsidiary powers essential to the preparation for and the effective prosecution of war, would exist and their complete exercise devolve upon that government, *ex necessitate*, even if the Constitution had been silent on the subject. The right to carry on war is a necessary and inherent right of all sovereign nations, to which they may be obliged to appeal in order to avoid destruction. The effect of the enumeration of these powers in the Constitution, therefore, is not to vest them in the general government so much as it is to prescribe the manner of their exercise, or to designate the specific agencies of the government upon whom they shall devolve. A declaration of war, for example, is generally a matter for the executive. It is the King of England, and not Parliament, who possesses the power. Parliament, by reason of its control of the purse, may exercise a restraining or even a controlling influence, and, thereby, delay or prevent a declaration of war by the King; but Parliament can neither directly declare nor directly prevent a declaration of war. The framers of our Constitution, however, concluded, and I think wisely, that such a power in the hands of a single person was not consonant with the genius and spirit of a republic such as ours. They, therefore, provided that Congress, and not the President, should have the sole power to declare war. The effect of this, as already suggested, is not to confer a power on the general government which otherwise would not exist, but to point out the department of that government upon whom the duty and responsibility of exercising the power shall rest. The period of deliberation having passed and the people, through their chosen representatives, having determined upon war, vigorous and effective action must ensue, to the end that the conflict may be speedily and successfully prosecuted. Here, singleness of command and concentration of power are vitally essential, and so the power to wage war is given to the President as Commander-in-Chief, and not to Congress.

The war powers vested in Congress and the war powers vested in the President, by virtue of his office as Commander-in-Chief, are distinct. Generally speaking, the war powers of the President under the Constitution are simply those which belong to any Commander-in-Chief of the military forces of a nation at war. *The Constitution confers no war powers upon the President as such.* Whatever war powers he possesses under the Constitution—that is, without legislative authority—he has, not because he is President, but because he is Commander-in-Chief. As Commander-in-Chief he has no greater or additional power because he is also President. This is a distinction which has been frequently overlooked and because not always borne in mind has led to much confusion of thought. It will tend to a more distinct understanding of the President's powers and limitations as Commander-in-Chief, if we will leave out of consideration altogether the fact that he is President, and think of him as a person who holds the military office only. As President he is the Executive department of the government, authorized to grant reprieves and pardons; in connection with the senate, to make treaties and appoint officers; to inform Congress, from time to time, as to the state of the Union; to recommend such measures of legislation as he deems necessary and expedient; to convene the Houses of Congress, or either of them on extraordinary occasions; to adjourn Congress in case of disagreement between the Houses as to the time of adjournment; to receive ambassadors and other public ministers; to commission all the officers of the United States, and take care that the laws be faithfully executed. All these duties relate, primarily, to a condition of peace; that is, they do not contemplate war as a basis for their exercise, though, of course, they may be exercised in time of war as well as in time of peace. He does not, however, command the military forces of the United States as President but as Commander-in-Chief. The two offices bear no necessary relation to one another, and the power to be exercised in the one office is in no manner amplified, restricted, or affected by the circumstance that the same person also occupies the other office. When war has been declared by Congress, the duty and power of waging war immediately attaches to the office of Commander-in-Chief, not to the office of President. Many persons are in the habit of thinking of the President as possessing extensive war powers, simply because he is President in time of war, but, I repeat, such war powers are his by virtue of being Commander-in-Chief, and not by virtue of being President. The office of Commander-in-Chief, having been created by the Constitution without prescribing the functions and powers to be exercised, it necessarily results that these are to be determined by ascertaining what functions and powers are recognized by the laws of war as belonging to that office; and when these have been ascertained, the line which separates the war powers of Congress from the war powers of the Commander-in-Chief will have been fixed. On the one side of this line Congress is supreme, and on the other side the Commander-in-Chief is supreme; and neither may lawfully invade the province of the other. Whatever any

Commander-in-Chief may do under the laws and practices of war as recognized and followed by civilized nations, may be done by the President as Commander-in-Chief. In carrying on hostilities he possesses sole authority, and is charged with sole responsibility, and Congress is excluded from any direct interference. In the command of the military forces, and in the conduct of the military operations, he may adopt any means, or follow any plan or method his judgment, or the judgment of his advisers and military subordinates, may approve, subject to the single restriction that he do not transcend the rules and usages of war authorized and recognized by the law of nations.

The office of President has grown in potency and influence to an extent never dreamed of by those who framed and adopted the Constitution. Even in normal times, Congress has been subjected to such a degree of executive domination as to threaten the stability of the principle of departmental independence involved in the distribution of the several powers among the three branches of government. There is a popular, ever-increasing disposition to regard the President as a superior officer rather than as a co-equal member of a tripartite organization. In times of public danger or disorder this tendency is greatly accentuated, and it is under all conditions a matter for serious concern, fraught with grave suggestions of peril. In great crises, the people not only turn to him as their natural leader, which he is, but they are coming more and more to regard him as the sole repository of their power which, very decidedly, he is not. With the advent of war, he is clothed, by the popular imagination, not only with all the imposing habiliments of military leadership, which are his by right, but with the rôle of virtual political dictatorship as well, an investment of power no President should ever be allowed to assume, and a burden of responsibility no President should ever be called upon to bear.　The danger from such a situation is that Congress will be driven from its traditional and constitutional place in public thought, as a co-ordinate branch of the government, with the unfortunate result that subordination and obedience will tend to replace common counsel and team work.　Of course, in time of war, the chief reliance must be the President, and every power which will aid in the successful prosecution of the war should be freely and promptly given him by Congress, not because the President demands it, but because, in the judgment of both Congress and the President, it is wise and expedient that it should be granted. But the possession of power carries with it corresponding responsibility.　The war powers, with the exception of those pertaining to the office of Commander-in-Chief, are vested in Congress, and that body must exercise its own judgment with respect to the extent and character of their use.　The advice and counsel of the President should be given great weight, but the acceptance of the President's recommendations must be the result of intelligent approval and not of blind obedience.　Any other course involves a double betrayal of official trust —usurpation of power by the President and abdication of duty on the part of Congress.

In the actual conduct of military operations, in the field where the battles are being fought, in the movement, disposition and discipline of the land and naval forces, the Commander-in-Chief is supreme. His will is law; his decisions are final, subject to review or reversal at the hand of no earthly power. He embodies in his single person the majesty and power of the Nation itself. In the territory of the enemy, occupied by the forces under his command, he may govern according to his discretion. He may supplant political institutions with military governors; put martial law, administered by soldiers, in the place of municipal law, administered by courts. The usages and laws of war alone, and not the Constitution of the United States, fix the limits of his authority. Outside the field of actual military operations, however, he has only the powers of the Chief Executive as enumerated and limited in the Constitution. The soldier or the spy he may try at the drum head and shoot at dawn; the citizen is under the protection of the guarantees of peace and subject only to the civil laws of the land.

The President is, of course, Commander-in-Chief of the Army and Navy at all times; but in time of peace his activities are limited to matters of routine, such as the acquisition and distribution of munitions and military supplies, the location and movement of officers and men, and the building, equipment, and movement of vessels. Only in time of war is it possible to bring into activity the real war powers which attach to his military office. The war powers of Congress, on the other hand, may be as completely utilized in time of peace as in time of war, though, of course, they never are. The fact remains, however, that the actual existence of war is not a necessary prerequisite for Congressional action of any kind, since the function of Congress is to provide rules of action to be put into execution by others. Statutes may be formulated and enacted, in time of peace, covering every conceivable contingency likely to arise in time of war, to be enforced, whenever conditions render them applicable, precisely as in the case of laws generally. It is, therefore, quite inaccurate to say that the powers of Congress are enlarged by the advent of war; that Congress may enact legislation at such a time which it would be without power to enact at another time. A state of war simply furnishes an occasion for the application of laws which are entirely valid in normal times but lack appropriate conditions for making them operative.

Of course, it is not possible in time of peace to anticipate, by legislation, the multitude of contingencies which will arise in time of war, and so as a matter of practical necessity, legislation under the war powers of Congress must await, in large measure, the course of events, inasmuch as the character and extent of such legislation must depend upon the necessities of war, as these necessities, from time to time, are developed. This situation, however, is one which is due to the limitations of human foresight and not to the nature of the power or the state of affairs to be affected.

An important power which belongs to the Commander-in-Chief is that of governing enemy territory actually occupied by his forces. He not only has complete and exclusive authority over such territory during the progress of hostilities, but he may continue to maintain a military government after hostilities have ceased; otherwise conditions of great disorder might prevail, pending the establishment of civil government by Con-

gress. By the conquest and occupation of enemy territory, the government previously existing is, *ipso facto*,
overthrown, and, from the necessity of the case, in order
that anarchy may be prevented, lawlessness restrained,
private property protected, and the lives and liberties
of the inhabitants safeguarded, the military commander
of the successful armies must have power to maintain
temporarily such government as the exigencies of the
situation may require. Thus, when New Mexico was
occupied by our armies in 1846, General Kearny, in
accordance with this rule, and under the authority of
the Commander-in-Chief, established a provisional government which, in turn, enacted laws, instituted courts,
and administered the civil affairs of the inhabitants.
This government remained in operation after the termination of hostilities and its acts were confirmed as lawful by the Supreme Court.[1]

During the existence of a state of belligerency, the
will of the military commander within occupied enemy
territory is absolute. As forcibly stated by counsel for
the government in the Milligan case:

"The officer executing martial law is at the same time supreme
legislator, supreme judge, and supreme executive. As necessity
makes his will the law, he only can define and declare it; and whether
or not it is infringed, and of the extent of the infraction, he alone
can judge; and his sole order punishes or acquits the alleged offender."[2]

This is called martial law, but, obviously, it is not
law at all, for law implies uniformity, permanency, uni-
versality. Martial law is simply the arbitrary will of the

[1] 20 How. 176.
[2] 4 Wall 2.

Commander, exercised without reference to any principle and subject to no limitation or, as said by Sir Matthew Hale, "something indulged, rather than allowed as a law."

But the power, whatever it may be called, is one which finds no limitations in the Constitution, or in the general laws of the land. Its arbitrary and absolute character is shown by the ancient maxim by which it is characterized: "The will of the conqueror is the law of the conquered." The harshness of this ancient rule, in actual practice, has long since passed away. As administered under the usages of modern and civilized nations, martial law, or, more accurately speaking, military government, is tempered by the dictates of fairness and humanity, and kept, as far as possible, within the bounds of necessity; the civil rights of the inhabitants are interfered with as little as possible; and the municipal laws, at the time in force within the occupied territory, are followed and enforced unless they tend to interfere with the prosecution of military operations, or the accomplishment of the objects for which the warfare was inaugurated. Nevertheless, as long as actual warfare continues, the ancient maxim is the yard-stick by which the power is ultimately measured.

The Supreme Court of the United States has said:

"In such cases the conquering power has a right to displace the pre-existing authority, and to assume, to such extent as it may deem proper, the exercise by itself of all the powers and functions of government. It may appoint all the necessary officers and clothe them with designated powers, larger or smaller, according to its pleasure. It may prescribe the revenues to be paid, and apply them to its own use or otherwise. It may do anything necessary to strengthen itself and weaken the enemy. There is no limit to the powers that may be exerted in such cases, save those which are found in the laws and usages of war." [3]

When peace has been restored, the severity of this rule of absolute power is abated, but the authority of the Commander-in-Chief to administer the government of conquered territory still continues until Congress shall have assumed control. This is in accordance with the precedents of our own history and is sanctioned by the general custom of nations. Military government having been instituted in accordance with the usages of war, will continue at the pleasure of the conqueror. It does not end with the cessation of hostilities. Indeed, it is not practicable that it should do so, since there must necessarily be a period of time, after warfare has ended, before civil government can be established and, in the meantime, government being a necessity of civilized existence, the Commander-in-Chief as the representative of the conqueror must continue to govern until superseded by other lawful authority. Inasmuch, however, as one of the chief purposes of a military government has been achieved, namely, the successful prosecution of military operations, the power of the military commander will be adjusted to that fact and curtailed accordingly. His authority is no longer utilized to promote warfare but to preserve order, safeguard property, protect life; in short, to administer the ordinary affairs of a civil population. As a natural consequence, therefore, his power is lessened since the necessity for its unlimited exercise no longer exists. The power itself remains, but diminished in extent and

[3] 20 Wall 387, 394.

changed in quality to conform to the altered conditions. The military commander still governs; but he administers the laws of peace and not of war.

The length of time during which military government shall be allowed to continue over conquered and acquired territory after the conclusion of a treaty of peace, is a matter wholly for political determination, in no manner controlled or affected by the Constitution, or subject to judicial review or determination. After the acquisition of the Spanish possessions, only a short time intervened until the establishment of civil government. In the case of the territory acquired from Mexico, several months elapsed before Congress took action in that respect. In the case of Porto Rico, a military government continued for a year after the acquisition, although conditions had been entirely peaceful during the whole of that time. In the Philippines, a much longer time elapsed; but there, of course, the situation was altogether different. After the treaty of Paris, which was ratified and proclaimed on April 11, 1899, the Islands were in a state of insurrection, which continued to be more or less serious for about a year, by which time organized opposition to the authority of the United States ceased, although a species of guerilla warfare persisted for some time longer. It was not, however, until March 2, 1900, that Congress took the first steps looking to the establishment of a government by legislative authority. Even then, a civil government was not established by Congress, but provision was made for a continuance of government by the President. The so-called Spooner amendment to the army appropriation bill of that date, provided that:

"All military, civil and judicial powers necessary to govern the Philippine Islands . . . shall, until otherwise provided by Congress, be vested in such person or persons and shall be exercised in such manner as the President of the United States shall direct," etc.

The only effect of this legislation was, probably, to put an end, at least technically, to the military government, created and administered by the Commander-in-Chief, and substitute a quasi civil government, created and administered by the President. The only immediate action which resulted was a laconic cable from the Secretary of War to the Philippine Commission, in the following words: "Until further orders government will continue under existing instructions and orders." And under this amendment to an appropriation bill and this somewhat imperious telegram from the War Department, the ten million inhabitants of the Philippine archipelago were governed for many months.

The President continued to administer the affairs of the Islands, under the authority of this amendment, until July, 1902, when Congress finally passed the Philippine Organic Act, providing for a complete system of civil government. It will be seen, therefore, that after the acquisition, the Philippines were governed under the war powers of the Commander-in-Chief, for a period of nearly two years, and by the Chief Executive, under a legislative power, for a year longer.

Our acquisition and control of the Philippines constitute not only an interesting and notable development of our national policies, but afford a striking example of the powers of the President as Commander-in-Chief and of the flexible quality of the powers of

Congress to govern new territory. The acquisition itself and every step taken for the pacification and government of the inhabitants were savagely assailed, as being contrary to the genius of our institutions and opposed to the plain provisions and principles of the Constitution.

However, not only have events fully justified our retention of these possessions—and it is difficult to imagine how we could have done otherwise, without a deplorable exhibition of national weakness if not dishonor—but the various steps for their government taken by the Commander-in-Chief, and by the President, have been completely approved and ratified by Congress, and their validity sustained by the Supreme Court.

The distinction between the military government established and carried on under the war powers of the Commander-in-Chief, and the subsequent government by the President, is quite clearly recognized by the Philippine Organic Act, the first section of which ratifies the action of the President in creating the Philippine Commission and conferring authority upon it, by the executive order of June 21, 1901, which was made under the authority of the Spooner amendment, and the second section of which ratifies the action of the President, taken by virtue of the authority vested in him as Commander-in-Chief of the Army and Navy, as set forth in his order of July 12, 1898.

The nature and extent of the power to declare and enforce martial law, has, from time to time, engaged the attention of the Houses of Congress and of the courts, and has received earnest consideration at the hands of distinguished legal and political writers. It is not difficult to state, in general terms, what the power is; the definition is startlingly simple. As already suggested, martial law is not *law* at all; it is simply the arbitrary will of the military commander, tempered, in practice, by a more or less humane regard for the actual necessities of the existing situation. To state, however, what circumstances will justify its application, is a more difficult task. The power of the military commander to rule within the occupied territory of a belligerent enemy has just been spoken of. But this, according to high authority, is the establishment of military government rather than of martial law, a distinction which is both technically accurate and practical, since the former is operative within enemy territory and the latter within our own boundaries.

Chief Justice Chase, in the Milligan case, said there were, under the Constitution, three kinds of military jurisdiction: one to be exercised both in peace and war; another to be exercised in time of foreign war outside the United States, or in time of revolution and civil war within the rebellious states or districts; and the third to be exercised in time of invasion or insurrection within the boundaries of the United States, or, during revolution, within the states adhering to the national government, when the public danger requires its exercise.[4]

The learned Justice goes on to say that the warrant for the exercise of the first of these is to be found in the acts of Congress, which provide for the government of the national forces and prescribe rules and articles of

[4] 4 Wall 141.

war; that the second may be distinguished as military government, taking the place of local law and exercised by the military commander, but under the direction of the President, with the express or implied sanction of Congress; and that it is only the third which may be properly denominated martial law; and this may be called into action by Congress, or, temporarily, when the action of Congress cannot be had, or where justified or excused by the peril, by the President, in times of insurrection or invasion or of civil or of foreign war in localities where ordinary law no longer adequately secures public safety and private rights.

This analysis of military jurisdiction and definition of martial law is contained in a minority opinion, which though not dissenting from the conclusions of the majority, differs from the opinion of the majority in some particulars. It will be seen from this opinion that martial law may be called into operation either by the action of Congress, or by that of the President. While the opinion does not so declare, it would seem clear that the power, when exercised by the Executive as an original power, is by virtue of his office of Commander-in-Chief, and not of President. But, whether exercised by that officer directly, or under enabling legislation, or by Congress directly—if and when that be possible —it is the Commander-in-Chief who enforces martial law, and it is the will of the Commander-in-Chief alone which measures the limits of its enforcement.

In the majority opinion delivered by Mr. Justice Davis, the power of a military commander to establish martial law within the lines of his military district, outside the zone of actual invasion or military operations, is vigorously challenged. The Court said:

"Martial law cannot arise from a threatened invasion. The necessity must be actual and present; the invasion real such as effectually closes the courts and deposes the civil administration." [5]

The Court proceeds to say that if in case of foreign invasion, or civil war, the courts are closed, and it be impossible to administer criminal justice according to law, then, on the theater of actual military operations, where war prevails, and the necessity exists to furnish a substitute for the civil authority, it is allowable to govern by martial rule until the laws can again have their free course.

"Martial rule can never exist where the courts are open and in the proper and unobstructed exercise of their jurisdiction. It is also confined to the locality of actual war." [6]

It would seem, therefore, in case of foreign war, waged entirely beyond the boundaries of the United States, the occasion for a declaration of martial law within our boundaries could never legitimately arise.

This decision, and, more particularly, the majority opinion, in the beginning, was adversely and severely criticised by many of the loyal men of the North. It was denounced as usurpation, as dangerous to the lives and liberties of loyal citizens, and subversive of a free people's will. There were even threats of impeaching the judges. But with the lapse of time and the consequent subsidence of the passions aroused by the Civil War, the enduring wisdom and justice of the decision

[5] 4 Wall 127.
[6] 4 Wall 127.

have come to be generally recognized. It constitutes
one of the finest, among many, examples of the intellectual honesty and judicial courage of that great tribunal. If the political structure erected by the Fathers
rests upon any one pillar more securely than upon
another, it is upon that which upholds the right of the
individual to invoke the judgment of the civil courts
of the land upon his conduct. Presentment to, and
trial and judgment by, judicial authority is fundamental
in our system of jurisprudence, as it is in every other
having its roots in the common law. These are rights
so sacred and imperative, so vital to the continued
efficacy of free institutions, that nothing short of overwhelming and inevitable necessity can ever justify
their suspension. So long as that necessity does not
arise, the promoters of disloyalty, in common with other
malefactors, must be left to the deliberate processes
of the courts; but whenever the necessity does arise,
and the hand of civil authority is no longer effective,
the arm of military power may be, and must be, invoked
for swift and relentless action. When the Nation is
fighting for its life, many things, even things of great
moment, may wait; but at such a time, above all other
times, there can be no vacillating truce—no weak and
dubious parley—with the forces of disloyalty: *then* if
the judge cannot act, the soldier must.

It must never be forgotten that this is a government
of laws, under which the conduct of the individual must
conform to general, definite and pre-established rules—
not to the opinions of other men. To substitute the
will of a military commander for the *law* of the land, is
a step so drastic that it may be taken, even in time of

actual war, only when necessary to "preserve the safety of the army and society." It is a power, which, in this country, it would seem, may be exercised by the national government alone, since only that government may declare or recognize a state of public war. So-called martial law in a state of the Union can never, legitimately, be anything more than the use of the military forces as an enlarged *posse comitatus* to assist the civil authorities in suppressing disorder and enforcing the laws of the state. No conceivable circumstances, in my judgment, can ever warrant the governor, as commander of the state militia, in supplanting the statutes of the state by the will of a military commander or commission, as was actually done in one of the states in recent years. If the disorder be so great that the state authorities can no longer cope with it, the remedy is to invite the aid of the national government, under Article IV, Section 4, of the Constitution, which obliges the United States to protect each state against invasion and, when called upon, against domestic violence. In the improbable event that the situation does not yield to this power, the question of war and of martial rule will become a matter for the national and not the state government to deal with.

Closely allied, and sometimes corollary, to the power to declare martial law, is the power to suspend the privilege of the writ of habeas corpus. The Constitution neither guarantees this ancient writ, nor expressly provides for its suspension. As one of the great charters of English constitutional liberty, it accompanied the colonists from the old world to the new and formed part of the common law of the various states after the success of the Revolution. The only provision of the national Constitution referring to the writ is that contained in the second clause of Section 9, Article I, which provides:

"The privilege of the writ of habeas corpus shall not be suspended unless when in cases of revolution or invasion the public safety may require it."

This provision implies the existence of the writ and conclusively assumes the authority of the courts to issue it, since it necessarily involves a judicial inquiry. It will be observed, also, that the Constitution does not *expressly authorize* the suspension of the writ. It *assumes* the power and limits the occasions for its exercise. Before the privilege of the writ can be suspended, not only must there be revolution or invasion of the territory of the United States but, in addition, the public safety must require the suspension.

Under the English practice the Habeas Corpus Act, itself, is suspended, with the result that the writ may not be issued at all. Our Constitution refers to the *privilege* of the writ and contemplates that the privilege, and not the writ itself, is to be suspended. The effect of this is that, under our practice, after a suspension, the writ may still issue, but relief must be denied upon showing a suspension of the privilege within the terms of the Constitution.

The suspension has no affirmative effect. It makes no one subject to arrest or imprisonment, who would not otherwise be liable. It does not put into operation martial law, or deprive the citizen of any right which he would have in the orderly and ordinary administration of the law. It simply prevents relief under this

summary and historic remedy. The accused must still
be proceeded against by presentment and indictment,
and is entitled to a speedy and public trial with all its
constitutional incidents.

Does the power to suspend the writ pertain to the
office of the Commander-in-Chief or must it be exercised or authorized by Congress? This question has
met with a variety of answers from statesmen, legal
and political writers, and the courts. The Supreme
Court of the United States, in an early decision,
assumed that the power belonged to Congress. In the
early days of the Civil War, President Lincoln proceeded upon the theory that it was a power which he
might exercise as Commander-in-Chief, and he acted
accordingly. His conclusion, however, was directly
challenged by Chief Justice Taney, who held that it
was a power vested alone in Congress. Thereafter
Congress itself apparently accepted that view, and on
March 3, 1863, passed an act, by the terms of which
the President was authorized to suspend the privilege
of the writ, whenever, in his judgment, the public safety
required it. The act contained various provisions limiting the effect of the suspension and regulating the
authority of the courts in dealing with cases arising
under it. It would seem now to be established by the
weight of authority that the power is one which belongs
to Congress, but which Congress may delegate to the
President. At any rate, in view of the legislation devolving the authority upon the President and the
general acquiescence in the validity of the act, the
question may be regarded as no longer open to practical
dispute.

CHAPTER V

THE WAR POWERS—EXTENT AND LIMITATIONS

The last preceding lecture dealt with the nature of the war powers under the Constitution, the fundamental basis upon which they rest, and their division between Congress and the Commander-in-Chief. We have now to inquire in respect of their extent and whether they are subject to any, and, if any, what limitations.

No decision of the Supreme Court, perhaps, has provoked more earnest expressions of approval, upon the one hand, and of disapproval, upon the other, than that in which a majority of the judges concurred in the second Legal Tender case. The majority of the Court, in a former decision, had held the Legal Tender Acts unconstitutional. We are all familiar with the history of the events which culminated in the partial reconstitution of that tribunal, by which a majority, denying the validity of these acts, became a majority, affirming their validity. I am one of those who thoroughly approve the later decision. It is one of the great legal chapters in the history of constitutional development, which recounts the progressive steps by which the theory of a Federation of states has been absorbed in the realization of a Nation. It is not only a model of clear judicial reasoning, but a superb example of that judicial statesmanship of which the unique powers exercised by the Supreme Court have furnished many instances.

In the course of the opinion written by Mr. Justice Strong, it is said:

"It is not to be denied that acts may be adapted to the exercise of lawful power, and appropriate to it, in seasons of exigency which would be inappropriate at other times."

Attention is then directed to the fact that at the time Congress attempted to make treasury notes a legal tender, the country was in the midst of a civil war which threatened the overthrow of the government and the destruction of the Constitution. The public treasury was empty, the credit of the government well nigh exhausted. Specie payment had been suspended. Taxation was inadequate to pay interest on the debt already incurred, and it was impossible to await the collection of additional taxes. The armies were unpaid to the extent of many millions of dollars. Trade was threatened with paralysis. Foreign credit was gone, and confidence in the ability of the general government to save the Union and itself, hung trembling in the balance. It was at such a crisis in our affairs, and under such conditions of compelling necessity, that Congress passed the Legal Tender Acts. As already stated, the action of Congress, having been first annulled, was then upheld. Mr. Justice Strong, in passing upon the question, after reciting the facts just stated, said:

"Now, if it were certain that nothing else would have supplied the absolute necessities of the Treasury, that nothing else would have enabled the government to maintain its armies and navy, that nothing else would have saved the government and the Constitution from destruction, while the Legal Tender Acts would, could any one be bold enough to assert that Congress transgressed its powers? Or if these enactments did work these results, can it be maintained now that they were not for a legitimate end, or 'appropriate and adapted to that end', in the language of Chief Justice Marshall? That they did work such results is not to be doubted. Something revived the drooping faith of the people; something brought immediately to the government's aid the resources of the nation, and something enabled the successful prosecution of the war, and the preservation of the national life. What was it, if not the legal tender enactments?"

The sword and the purse are the two indispensable requisites of war. In time of war, when the life of the Nation is at stake, the power of the general government to sharpen and strengthen the one, and fill the other, and utilize them both, by any means and in any way the authorized agencies of that government may determine, cannot admit of question; and, in my judgment, the power exists without any restrictions whatsoever, save those which are imposed by such express prohibitions of the Constitution, and such fundamental restraints upon governmental action, as are obviously and clearly intended to apply at all times and under all conditions.

There is, in this field of governmental activity, therefore, little, if any occasion to employ those niceties of logical analysis which have been crystalized into canons of statutory and constitutional construction, the application of which tends to elucidate the meaning of language otherwise obscure. We are not now dealing with those powers of government which have to do with our ordinary affairs, and whose extension or restriction is important only as it bears upon the comfort or the convenience or the efficiency of society. We are dealing with those vital powers, the employment of which may become essential to our continued existence as a people. It is manifest that in determining the extent of such powers as these, we shall be justified in making assumptions and indulging in constructions which could not be tolerated in respect of normal matters. We may safely deny to the general government indifferent powers, or even important powers, if they concern only our ordinary relations with one another; but to deny to the general government any power essential to the preservation of the Nation, is to gamble with the forces of life and death, and to court irreparable disaster. The Constitution looks to an enduring Republic and a perpetual Union made "more perfect." This the Framers intended, and for this many thousands of brave men have perished. To hold that men may be called upon to die for these ends, but that the general government lacks any conceivable power to attain them by means which will entail other and lesser sacrifices, would be to convert the Constitution from a charter of human liberty into a deadly ambush. No such ghastly paradox can be admitted. The powers of the general government are completely adequate. If the Republic shall ever fall—if our people shall ever be conquered by a foreign foe—if the Union shall ever be destroyed—it will be because we lack the will or the strength to fight, and not because our government lacks authority to utilize every resource of the Nation for its preservation. If, however, it should, unfortunately, transpire that there are some things, the doing of which should become vital to the successful prosecution of a future war, but which, under some contracted view of national power, are held to lie within the restraints of the Constitution, we may be confronted with the alternative of violating the Constitution, or sacrificing the Republic. In that unhappy event, we must, of course, determine which is the more important to be saved. I have as much reverence for the Constitution as anybody, and I should be as loath as any one to disregard its provisions, but, I suspect, in exercising my choice, I should be greatly influenced by the reflection that a fractured Constitution, however undesirable, would be a small disaster compared, for example, with a German victory! And while I have said this—and while I am sure no lover of his country could say less than this—it is said for the sake of emphasis, rather than for the purpose of intimating the possibility of such an alternative. On the contrary, the power of national self-preservation is implicit in every line and letter of the Constitution, since the continued existence of that instrument is wholly dependent upon the continued existence of the Nation whose Constitution it is. I repeat and apply the words of President Lincoln, in his letter to A. G. Hodges, April 8, 1864: "I felt that measures, otherwise unconstitutional, might become lawful by becoming indispensable to the preservation of the Constitution through the preservation of the Union."

The power to declare war includes every subsidiary power necessary to make the declaration effective. It does not mean power to wage war feebly, with restricted means or limited forces. It means the power to proceed to the last extremity—to call to the service of the Nation every vestige of property and every drop of blood in the land. It is a power that, once invoked, admits of no limitations—tolerates no qualifications— except such as are of a more vital character than the imperious necessity with which they compete; for since defeat may entail the loss of all that a free people hold dear, a people worthy to be free can be supposed to intend no otherwise than that, if all must, indeed, be lost, the sacrifice shall follow a stern resistance and an exercise of power which recognizes *physical* limitations alone.

John Quincy Adams, speaking of the war power, said: "This power is tremendous; it is strictly constitutional; but it breaks down every barrier so anxiously erected for the protection of liberty, of property and of life."

Our government was created for the problems of war, as well as for those of peace, and it possesses powers appropriate for either state. Having no relation to the *conditions* of peace, the war powers, at such a time, are wholly subordinate to the *powers* of peace—not effaced, but lying dormant and potential. In time of war, the situation, in many respects, is reversed. As the highest duty of the Nation is self-preservation, the rights of peace must then be held in subjection to the necessities of war. This does not result in the suspension of the Constitution, as some have petulantly suggested, but it may result in a suspension of the constitutional rights of the individual, because they conflict with the paramount powers of war. It is difficult to point out, in advance, precisely which of these rights may be thus affected, or the extent of the interference, since the faculty of anticipation is limited. In a general way it may be said that as necessity is the occasion of the interference, it is also the standard by which the extent of it is to be determined. Whenever, therefore, the enforcement of these constitutional guaranties will interfere with the successful prosecution of the war—will put an obstacle in the way of the fighting forces of the Nation, or lessen their fighting ability—individual right must yield to the general and superior right of national defense. When the powers of war and the rights of peace become irreconcilable, both cannot stand, and it requires no argument to demonstrate that in such case the rights of the individual, rather than the common welfare, must be sacrificed. *Salus populi suprema est lex.* Except, however, as an assertion of these rights may conflict with the operation of the war powers, they are still in full force, to be invoked by the citizen and enforced by the courts, in war as completely as in peace. But individual privilege and individual right, however dear or sacred, or however potent in normal times, must be surrendered by the citizen to strengthen the hand of the government lifted in the supreme gesture of war. Everything that he has, or is, or hopes to be—property, liberty, life—may be required. In time of peace, an attempt to interfere with the least of these would be, and ought to be, resisted to the utmost. In time of war, when the Nation is in deadly peril, every freeman, who prizes the boon of *enduring* liberty, will lay them all, freely and ungrudgingly, upon the sacrificial altar of his country.

And so, freedom of speech may be curtailed or denied, in order that the morale of the population and the fighting spirit of the army may not be broken by the preachers of sedition; freedom of the press interfered with, in order that our military plans and movements may not be made known to the enemy; deserters and spies put to death, without indictment or trial by jury;

private mills and mines taken over and operated by the government; supplies requisitioned; property of alien enemies lawfully in the country and normally under the protection of the Constitution, seized without judicial process and converted to the public use without "due process of law"; food supplies, fuel, raw materials, useful in the manufacture of requisites of war, conserved, or their production stimulated, by price fixing or regulation of consumption; transportation systems, telegraph and telephone lines taken possession of and operated by the national government; and a multitude of other powers, the exercise of which in time of peace would be intolerable and inadmissible, may be employed, by or under the direction of Congress, to meet the necessities and emergencies of war.

Not only are the ordinary and normal rights of the individual thus gravely affected, but the line, which in time of peace separates the national from the state powers, is thrust aside by the enactment of national statutes postponing rights and suspending remedies under state laws, where their immediate enforcement might interfere with military operations. Thus, in order that persons in the military service of the United States may not be prejudiced or injured in their civil rights during their term of service, and to enable them to devote their entire energy to the military needs of the Nation, Congress has enacted that, during the continuance of the present war, certain legal proceedings and transactions affecting such persons, shall be suspended. Under this act, for example, before judgment by default can be entered, the plaintiff must file an affidavit showing that the defendant is not in the military service, or, if unable to do that, an affidavit to the effect that defendant is in the service or that plaintiff is unable to determine the fact either way. If defendant be in the service, or that fact be left undetermined, counsel for the absent defendant must be appointed to protect his interests.

If judgment shall be finally rendered against defendant, and it afterward appear that he was prejudiced by reason of his military service in making his defense, judgment may thereafter be set aside in the manner and upon the conditions provided in the act. Provision is also made by which proceedings, in any action to which a person in military service is a party, may be stayed during the period of service and for a limited time thereafter. Courts in which such actions are brought are also authorized to stay execution of judgment and to vacate or stay attachments or garnishments. Eviction or distress is forbidden during military service except upon leave of Court where the agreed rent does not exceed $50 per month, and where the premises are occupied chiefly for dwelling purposes by dependents of the defendant. These provisions, so far as they are applicable to the state courts, would, of course, be entirely beyond the peace powers of Congress, but are justified under its war powers, since, by preventing the diversion of men in military service from their military duties, the efficiency of the army is materially increased.

By another act it is made an offense to set up or keep certain disorderly houses in proximity to military camps, etc., within zones established by the Secretary of War, a subject which in time of peace falls wholly under the police powers of the state. The act has been attacked as an invasion of these reserved powers of the state, but has been sustained as a legitimate exercise of the war powers.[1]

The power to declare war carries with it, by necessary implication, the power to employ any appropriate means to render the declaration effective, that is, to wage war speedily and victoriously. It is apparent that good order, morality, sobriety, health and subordination not only contribute to the well-being of the army, but are vitally essential to its efficiency; hence anything which adds to, or tends toward preserving, these qualities, promotes the success of our armies; and it follows that Congress may, under its war powers, command whatever will effect or aid in effecting these results, or forbid whatever will interfere with their attainment. The power which is exercised by Congress in this instance is not the police power, since it is not exercised to the end and for the ultimate purpose of safeguarding the health or morals of the persons affected, but it is exercised as a means to the end, and for the ultimate purpose, of increasing the efficiency of the fighting forces of the Nation.

The war powers are wholly distinct from the police powers, although their exercise may, and frequently does, bring about similar results.

Perhaps no statute passed by Congress during the present war was more strenuously opposed, in certain of its features, during its consideration, or more bitterly assailed since its enactment, than the so-called "Espionage Act." To my mind, however, no statute could

[1] 247 Red. Rep. 362.

be more plainly defensible, for if the utilization of the man power and resources of the country, to the utmost limit, be justified, in order to win the war, surely legislation which seeks to punish and prevent false statements calculated and intended to obstruct and delay or defeat the accomplishment of that end, must be sound and righteous. Instead of going too far, the Act did not go far enough. In time of peace, we may treat scurrilous and abusive criticisms of our form of government, our Constitution and our institutions with contempt alone; but in time of war—when every disloyal word, every profane criticism of our aims, our motives, our uniform, our flag, may, by delaying preparations or reducing the fighting will of the people, contribute to the sacrifice of men upon the battlefields—an unbridled tongue may be as dangerous as a wicked hand.

The provisions of the original Espionage Act were expanded and strengthened by the amendatory act of May 16, 1918, by which it is made an offense, severely punishable, to say or do anything, except by way of *bona fide*, and not disloyal, advice, to an investor or investors, with intent to obstruct the sale by the United States of bonds or other securities of the United States, or the making of loans by or to the United States; or to cause or incite, or attempt to cause or incite insubordination, etc., in the military forces of the United States; or obstruct or attempt to obstruct recruiting or enlisting; *or to wilfully utter, print, write or publish any disloyal, scurrilous or abusive language* about the form of government or Constitution of the United States, or the military or naval forces, or the flag of the United States, or the uniform of the army or navy, or any language intended to bring either of these into *contempt, scorn, contumely or disrepute;* or to utter, print, write, or publish any language intended to incite, provoke or encourage resistance to the United States, or *to promote the cause of its enemies;* or wilfully display the flag of any foreign enemy; or, by language spoken or written, to urge, incite or advocate any curtailment of the production of any thing or product essential to the prosecution of the war, with intent thereby to cripple or hinder the prosecution of the war by the United States; or to advocate, teach, defend or suggest the doing of any of the acts above enumerated. These provisions are comprehensive and impressive. They apparently leave no loophole of escape for the disloyal defamer of his country or its defenders, or the disloyal vilifier of the elementary things which symbolize its sovereignty, or for the aider or abetter of the enemy. They carry stern assurance that the Nation intends to protect itself against treachery at home, no less than against force from abroad.

The difficulty with the original act was that it applied only to false reports and statements made with intent to interfere with our military operations or success. The new law includes *disloyal utterances* designed to belittle and defile our institutions, the effect of which upon the *morale* of the people, while more insidious, may be none the less serious. Criticisms, levelled against the act on the ground that it unduly curtails freedom of speech and of the press, are wholly without justification. Criticism of the administration of government, of the conduct of the war, of the action, or lack of action, on the part of the President or any lesser official, is not forbidden. Such criticism, if truthful and timely and suggestive of appropriate remedies, may be greatly helpful. The act is directed against opprobrious language respecting matters which lie at the foundations of our national faith. Utterances of this character are reprehensible and deserving of unqualified condemnation at all times and under all circumstances—they are punished under state laws whenever they tend to create a breach of the peace—but in time of war they are essentially treasonable, and should be visited with social ostracism and severely substantial punishment. Any course less firm will not only encourage the disloyal but dishearten those who keep the faith in spirit and in fact. The order of President Lincoln, made under the Act of 1863, suspending the privilege of the writ of *habeas corpus* as to prisoners of war, spies, or aiders or abetters of the enemy, may be read with profit in this connection by those who condemn the present act as unnecessarily drastic. He there defined the aider or abetter of the enemy as "one who seeks to exalt the motives, character, and capacity of armed traitors—overrates the success of our adversaries or underrates our own—who seeks false causes of complaint against our government or inflames party spirit among ourselves and gives to the enemy that moral support which is more valuable to them than regiments of soldiers or millions of dollars."

The constitutionality of the Conscription Act passed by Congress under the power to "raise and support armies" was attacked, before its passage, in Congress, and has been attacked, since its enactment, in the courts. The legislation was assailed on the grounds, among others, that compulsory military service constituted involuntary servitude, and therefore violated the Thirteenth Amendment; that no power to provide for such service was granted by the Constitution; that the act was invalid in so far as it authorized the President to draft into the armies of the United States, for service abroad, members of the National Guard; and that there was no constitutional warrant for sending citizens to serve on foreign soil. The contention respecting involuntary servitude was so manifestly without merit, that it was speedily disposed of by the Supreme Court as being a "contention . . . refuted by its mere statement." The Thirteenth Amendment was directed against slavery or peonage, or other compulsory service involving some form or degree of slavery. It was never meant to include, and, of course, clearly, does not include, the constraint of military service for the common defense. Such service simply recognizes and discharges a reciprocal obligation implicit in citizenship. It does not constitute the servile subjection of a bondsman to a master, but the supreme requital of the freeman to the country which safeguards his liberties.

The claim that the Constitution contains no grant of power to provide for compulsory military service, and hence the act is invalid, is equally untenable. Chief Justice White, in the selective draft cases,[2] disposed of it in a few sentences, as terse as they are conclusive:

"But the proposition simply denies to Congress the power to raise armies which the Constitution gives. . .

"Further, it is said, the right to provide is not denied by calling for volunteer enlistments, but it does not and cannot include the

[2] 245 U. S. 366.

power to exact enforced military duty by the citizen. This, however, but challenges the existence of all power, for a governmental power which has no sanction to it and which therefore can only be exercised provided the citizen consents to its exercise is in no substantial sense a power. . . *It may not be doubted that the very conception of a just government and its duty to the citizen includes the reciprocal obligation of the citizen to render military service in case of need and the right to compel it."*

The power to compel military service by conscription is one which belongs to all independent nations as inherent in sovereignty and as essential to self-preservation. It is impossible to conclude that the framers of the Constitution intended to withold from the national government a power so vital. Nothing short of a precise prohibition in the Constitution could justify such a conclusion. The power to raise armies must include every well-recognized method in use at the time the Constitution was adopted; and conscription had not only been freely employed by all foreign nations, but had been resorted to by the colonists, and earnestly recommended more than once by the Federal Congress to the several states as a means to fill up their quotas. The precedents of our own history, since the adoption of the Constitution, all favor the existence of the power. Conscription was adopted as a means to raise armies upon both sides during the Civil War and sustained by the courts, both north and south. The Supreme Court of Pennsylvania, in passing upon the Conscription Act of the Civil War, uses language so pertinent and forceful that I cannot forbear making two or three brief extracts:

"We cannot conceive of a nation without the inherent power to carry on war. The defense of person and property is a right belonging by nature to the individual, and to every individual, and is not taken away by association. It, therefore, belongs to individuals in their collective capacity, whenever thus threatened or assailed. The Constitution, following the natural right, vests the power to declare war in Congress, the representatives of the people. It is noticeable that the Constitution recognizes this right as pre-existing, for it says, to declare war, which presupposes the right to make war. The power to declare war necessarily involves the power to carry it on, and this implies the means, saying nothing now of the express power 'to raise and support armies', as the provided means. . . The right to the means carries all the means in possession of the nation. Every able-bodied man is at the call of the government, for assuredly in making war, as there is no limit to the necessity, there can be no limit to the force to be used to meet it. Therefore, if the emergency require it, the entire military force of the nation may be called into service. But the power to carry on war, and to call the requisite force into service, inherently carries with it the power to coerce or draft. A nation without the power to draw forces into the field, in fact would not possess the power to carry on war. The power of war, without the essential means, is really no power; it is a solecism. Voluntary enlistment is founded in contract. A power to command differs essentially from a power to contract. The former flows from authority; the latter from assent. The power to command implies a duty to obey, but the essential element of contract is freedom to assent or dissent. It is clear, therefore, that the power to make war, without the power to command troops into the field, is impotent—in point of fact, is no governmental power, because it lacks the authority to execute itself." . . .

"But by so much more that the life of a nation is greater than the life of an individual, which may be taken to preserve it, so much greater is the high purpose of raising an army to preserve the nation than the protection of the rights of the individual. The minor purpose, when urged as a reason for the limitation, cannot therefore be allowed to control the meaning of the plain language used for the major purpose. Then the inherent powers of a nation to make war for self-preservation, carrying with them all the means of making war effective, the express power to declare war and to raise and support armies, coupled with the express power to pass all laws necessary and proper to carry those powers into effect, all unite in sustaining the power to raise armies by coercion, and these are in turn sustained by the high, vital, and essential purposes of the grant." [3]

The objection that the provisions of the act with reference to the state militia are invalid, was based upon the contention that, as the Constitution authorizes Congress "to provide for calling forth the militia to *execute the laws of the Union, to suppress insurrections and repel invasions*," the power cannot be exercised for other than the enumerated purposes. It was urged that, by the act in question, Congress had undertaken to conscript the militia for purposes beyond those specified in the Constitution. The answer to this, however, is that Congress did not undertake to call forth, or conscript, the state militia at all. The act provides for the draft of the *members* of the National Guard—which is, of course, the organized militia—who will, by another provision of the act, "from the date of their draft stand discharged from the militia." The draft, therefore, is not of the state militia as such, but of the *individuals* who for the time being happen to compose the militia. It has become a commonplace of constitutional construction that, whenever a power is conferred upon Congress, the selection of the means by which the power is to be effectuated is a matter wholly within the discretion of that body, and any means appropriate to the end, and not prohibited by the Constitution, may be adopted. The power to raise armies, therefore, carries with it the power to do so by any appropriate, unprohibited means. The fact that a person is enrolled

[3] 45 Pa. 238.

in the state militia does not affect his obligation as a citizen to render military service to the United States. This was true under the old Constitution, and it is more emphatically true since the Fourteenth Amendment, by which national citizenship is affirmatively declared, independently of and paramount to state citizenship. As well said by Judge Speer in a recent case: "Congress may summon to its army thus authorized every citizen of the United States. Since it may summon all, it may summon any." [4] A citizen is not beyond the arm of the general government because he is a member of the state militia, any more than because he is a policeman. He is summoned not as a militiaman or as a policeman, but as and because he is a citizen of, and owes primary allegiance to, the Nation.

The power to send citizens composing our military forces into foreign countries is established by the precedents of our history and the decisions of our courts. Our troops, even in time of peace, have carried the flag across the Pacific to China; and our victorious armies have gone into Tripoli, Mexico, Cuba, Porto Rico, and the Philippines. The present draft law has been sustained against all these and other attacks, by every court in which the matter has arisen, including the Supreme Court of the United States, and the question of its validity may be regarded as having been conclusively and permanently set at rest.

While Congress has no power to directly interfere with, or curtail the war powers of the Commander-in-Chief, that body may supplement and enlarge such powers or may create occasions for their exercise, as well

[4] 243 Fed. 997.

as for the exercise of the executive powers of the President. An illustration of the separate but dependent functions of these several governmental agencies, is afforded by the provisions respecting the state militia. The Constitution devolves upon Congress the duty to provide for calling forth the militia to "execute the laws of the Union, to suppress insurrections and repel invasions." In pursuance of this provision, Congress has provided that in case of invasion, or imminent danger of invasion from any foreign nation, and in case of rebellion, etc., the President may call forth such number of the militia as he may deem necessary. The power thus given by Congress is vested in the President, in his capacity as such, and not as Commander-in-Chief. When, however, the call has been made, and the militia are in the actual service of the United States, the constitutional functions of the Commander-in-Chief at once supersede the executive powers of the President, by virtue of that clause of the Constitution which makes him Commander-in-Chief of the state militia, when called into the service of the United States.

As already suggested, no war powers attach to the office of President by the direct force of the Constitution; but the President, in fact, exerts war powers of the most extensive character, since he is charged with the duty of executing or overseeing the execution of the laws made by Congress in pursuance of its powers, whether of war or of peace. The authority of the President, however, is wholly dependent upon the action of Congress. The power of initiation is vested in the latter, and not in the former, the more or less prevalent opinion to the contrary notwithstanding. In fact, with

reference to these powers, the Ex...
tially what Roger Sherman, in the Fr...
characterized as "Nothing more than
carrying the will of the legislature in...
the burden and responsibility of initiati...
Congress should make that body all the n...
and prompt to act. In carrying on war, the ...
both as President and Commander-in-Chief, ...
given a free, as well as a strong hand. The conting...
of war are limitless—beyond the wit of man to fore...
Vitally critical situations may suddenly arise; th...
country may be encompassed by unexpected dangers,
which must be faced at once; confronted with grave
and serious problems, which will not wait for deliberation, but must be solved by immediate action. To
rely upon the slow and deliberate processes of legislation, after the situation and dangers and problems have
arisen, may be to court danger—perhaps overwhelming
disaster. In recognition of this necessity, Congress has
already enacted legislation conferring upon the President emergency powers, to be exerted during the continuance of a state of war, of the most far-reaching
character. It is impracticable for me to do more than
enumerate, in general terms, some of these provisions;
but, following an admirable introduction dealing with
the war powers generally, they have been grouped and
analyzed, with explanatory and supplemental notes,
by Major J. Reuben Clark, Jr., formerly Solicitor of
the Department of State, and published by the government in a volume entitled "Emergency Legislation."

Major Clark shows that this legislation authorizes the
Federal Executive (generally the President directly) to

rcise control over, or take possession of, or title to, vate property by (a) confiscation, (b) requisition, or) regulation.

The powers of confiscation extend to vessels in the ports of the United States, where there is a failure to comply with any regulations or rules issued, or orders given, under the Espionage Act; or where the destruction or injury of any such vessel is wilfully caused or permitted; or where the use of such vessel is knowingly permitted as a place of resort for conspirators, or persons preparing to commit any offense against the United States, or in violation of treaties or obligations of the United States under the law of nations; and to vessels disposed of in violation of certain provisions of the Shipping Board Act. The power of confiscation likewise extends to arms, munitions of war, and articles exported or attempted to be exported in violation of law, or whenever there is probable cause to believe they are being, or are intended to be, so exported. The President, under the Espionage Act, is given comprehensive power to forbid the exportation of articles from the United States whenever he shall find that the public safety shall so require.

The term "requisition," as Major Clark points out, includes "the taking or use of private property for the belligerent necessities of a belligerent government," and the power may be exercised against enemies in occupied enemy territory, and against citizens in domestic territory. In the former case, the power is governed by the principles of international law, and in the latter case by the domestic law. The power is one well known and frequently exercised in our own history.

Major Clark divides the various acts of Congress into two classes: Those where the power of requisition is complete and those where it is incomplete.

The President is given power of "complete requisition" in the case of distilled spirits; the output of factories in which ships or war materials are built or produced; contracts for building or purchasing ships or producing war materials, where the power is to modify or cancel any such contracts; ships constructed or in process of construction, or any part thereof, or the charter of such ships; food, fuel, and other supplies necessary to the support of the Army, or maintenance of the Navy, or for the common defense, together with storage facilities for such supplies; land needed for fortifications, coast defenses, and military training camps, aviation purposes, naval purposes, and other military uses. Under the Food Control Act, the President is authorized to requisition, by judicial proceeding, any necessaries which have been hoarded, the same to be sold as the Court may direct. The President has likewise been authorized to take over the possession and title of all vessels within the jurisdiction of the United States, owned, in whole or in part, by corporations, citizens, or subjects of any nation with which the United States may be at war.

Under the head of "incomplete requisitions" the President has been authorized to place compulsory orders with manufacturers of materials required by the government, including ships and war materials; and the Secretary of War has been authorized to place compulsory preferential orders for arms or munitions, or necessary supplies or equipment for the Army. The

President has been further authorized, when, in his opinion, the common defense will be better provided for, or the war more efficiently prosecuted, to require producers of coal and coke to sell their products only to the United States, through an agency to be designated, such agency to regulate the resale of such coal and coke, and the prices thereof, and to establish regulations governing methods of production, shipment, distribution, and so on. Provision has also been made for the requisition of the use of plants for the manufacture of munitions or military supplies, or of ships or war materials; or for the building of ships, or manufacture of materials or necessaries for the support of the Army, or maintenance of the Navy, or any public use connected with the common defense. He is authorized to take over plants for the production of coal and coke; and to take possession and assume control of any system or systems of transportation.

Under the head of "powers of regulation" he is authorized to regulate, by a system of licensing, the importation, manufacture, storage, mining or distribution of any necessaries; the production of malt or vinous liquors from foods, fruits, food materials or feeds. It is made an offense, without the license of the President, to trade, or attempt to trade with the enemy, or an ally of the enemy, or to transport any enemy person, or to communicate with the enemy. He is authorized to regulate dealings in wheat, and to guarantee prices; to purchase, store and sell at reasonable prices flour, meal, beans, potatoes, etc.; to regulate production, sale, shipment, distribution and apportionment of coal and coke; to regulate stock exchanges, and to fix prices for wheat, coal and coke, and for storage, and for articles made under requisitioned foreign patents; to regulate the keeping of records of clearing-houses and in other cases. He is authorized to regulate exports; to allow, under certain limitations, the importation of tick infested cattle; to control the disposition of vessels owned by American citizens; to regulate imports; to supervise the press and censor all private communications; to require disclosures of enemy, or ally of enemy, officials, directors or stockholders, and disclosures by holders and custodians of property belonging to enemies.

In addition to all this he is authorized to make many other regulations; to institute investigations into the food supply, car service, clearing-houses, stock exchanges, and a variety of other matters.

It will thus be seen that Congress has invested the President with virtual dictatorship over an exceedingly wide range of subjects and activities—a grant of power which no free people would tolerate under normal conditions, but which, under the great emergency of war, has properly received unhesitating popular approval. The mere recital of this legislation, bare and incomplete as it is, presents to the imagination a deeply impressive picture of moral solidarity, stability and self-restraint, which affords comforting assurance of the enduring quality of democratic institutions, and bears eloquent and convincing testimony to the determination of the country to consummate the high adventure upon which it had entered, regardless of the restraints, losses or sacrifices that might be entailed.

CHAPTER VI

THE TREATY-MAKING POWER—GENERAL

The power to make treaties necessarily exists as an inherent attribute of sovereignty, since it is an indispensable prerequisite to the maintenance of international relations. To deny the power is to deny the sovereignty. The power is one which has never belonged to, nor been exercised by, the states of the Union separately. Prior to the Revolution, the colonies had no international status—all foreign relations, including the making of treaties, were maintained, exclusively, by the British government. The inhabitants of the colonies constituted not a separate people, but essentially an integrant of the British people. The revolution against the mother country was based on the ground that their rights as English subjects, rather than as individuals, had been violated. By the Declaration of Independence, they recognized their former allegiance to the British Crown, by declaring that they were thenceforth absolved from it. Even before the Declaration of Independence, steps had been taken looking to a political union. Delegates were appointed from the several colonies for the purpose of considering the differences which had arisen between them and the English government. These delegates constituted the Continental Congress, and, as such, exercised the various powers of external sovereignty, which have been heretofore enumerated.[1] While the Declaration of Independence was in process of being considered and formulated, the Congress appointed a Committee to prepare Articles of Confederation. These Articles were prepared, and after being debated and amended, were finally adopted by the Congress in 1777, and subsequently ratified by the authority of the legislatures of the several states. This instrument, feeble and unsatisfactory though it was, contemplated a permanent establishment with sovereign powers, for it was designated "Articles of Confederation and *Perpetual Union*," and distinctly declared the sole and exclusive power of the United States, through the government of the Union, namely, the Congress of the Confederation, to enter into treaties and alliances, and to send and receive ambassadors. The Treaty of Amity and Commerce with France was ratified by this Congress as early as May 4, 1778; and treaties with other governments were in like manner ratified prior to the adoption of the Constitution. In no instance was the treaty-making power ever exercised, or this essential attribute of sovereignty ever possessed, by any state separately. Governments come and go—hereditary rulers give place to elected rulers—allegiance changes—but sovereignty is immortal. It is never in suspension searching for a possessor. A political society cannot exist without a supreme will somewhere; so that when sovereignty ceases in one holder, it must, instantly, attach to another. When, therefore, sovereignty over the American colonies ceased to exist in the British Crown, it immediately passed to the states, not severally but in their united and corporate capacity,

[1] Chap. II, p. 37.

where it has ever since remained, being exercised, in turn, by the several governmental agencies which were constituted by the general authority. The treaty-making power then, like the war-making powers, has always been vested in the Nation, and exercised by national instrumentalities. The provisions respecting it in the Constitution, in so far as the respective powers of the states and the Nation are concerned, are purely declarative, and, in so far as the general government is concerned, are confirmative rather than creative. In accordance with the principles already discussed this power would have passed to the general government instituted by the Constitution, as the lineal successor of the preceding national agencies, in the absence of prohibitions or otherwise clearly evinced intention to the contrary. If denied to the national government, it would not have been among the reserved powers of the states, but would have been among those reserved to the people, and, hence, incapable of practical exercise, a situation, of course, quite incapable of being imagined. The treaty-making power is not, therefore, one of the powers delegated or surrendered by the several states, or by the people of the several states, since it was never theirs to relinquish. It is an original acquisition of the people of the United States in their national capacity, part and parcel of the general and exclusive sovereignty of the Nation over all external affairs, and since the Constitution, which might have denied it, does not deny it to the general government, it must be vested in that government from the inherent necessities of the case, as well as by the grants and implications of the Constitution. In either event it is, of course, held under and subject to all applicable limitations arising from that instrument.

Charles Henry Butler, whose painstaking and valuable researches are embodied in his comprehensive work on the Treaty-Making Power, gives it as his matured opinion: "That the treaty-making power of the United States, as vested in the Central Government, is derived not only from the powers expressly conferred by the Constitution, but that it is also possessed by that Government as an attribute of sovereignty." [2]

The conclusion, in this respect, is not without practical value. In one sense, it may be unimportant to ascertain the origin and basis of the power, since the existence of it is not questioned; but from another point of view, the fact is highly important, since, as will appear later, it will reflect light on the question of the extent of the power, and the nature and degree of the constitutional restraints upon its exercise.

In its usual meaning a treaty signifies "a compact between two or more independent nations with a view to the public welfare." [3]   But an international compact may not always be a treaty within the meaning of the constitutional provision, which requires the participation of the Senate. Thus under Section 3 of the Tariff Act of 1897, provision was made whereby the President was authorized to negotiate, and, apparently without the concurrence of the Senate, conclude, commercial agreements in respect of certain specified matters with foreign countries. The Supreme Court said that if such an agreement did not technically constitute a treaty

[2] Treaty-Making Power, Section 3.
[3] 2 Bouvier, Law Dictionary, 1136.

requiring ratification, it was, nevertheless, an international compact, and therefore a treaty within the meaning of the act allowing an appeal to the Supreme Court where the validity or construction of a treaty is drawn in question.[4] The President has been similarly authorized by statute, from time to time, to make international agreements respecting other matters.

Congress has, likewise, vested the power in the Postmaster-General, by and with the advice and consent of the President, to negotiate and conclude postal treaties and conventions with foreign countries, for the purpose of perfecting our foreign postal service. A similar power had, in fact, been exercised almost from the inception of the government—sometimes with the participation of the Senate and sometimes without it; and a large number of such compacts were entered into, although the authority to make postal *treaties* and *conventions* does not seem to have been conferred upon the Postmaster-General in precise terms until 1872.

In addition to these matters, the President, acting alone, has, from time to time, made settlement of claims of American citizens against foreign governments by diplomatic negotiation and agreement, or through arbitration. He also possesses, and has frequently exercised, the power, without the participation of the Senate, to sign protocols and *modi vivendi;* a protocol being simply an agreed adjustment of an international matter without the formality of a treaty and constituting only a moral obligation; and a *modus vivendi* being a temporary agreement concerning disputed matters pending the conclusion of a formal treaty. An inter-

[4] 224 U. S. 600.

national agreement may, therefore, be a treaty within the meaning of a statute, or under the general definition, or may be an international compact, without being a treaty within the technical meaning of the Constitution. Precisely where the dividing line is to be drawn has never been authoritatively determined, but so far as indicated by the instances referred to, international agreements which are not treaties in the full constitutional sense, are perhaps confined to such as affect administrative matters, as distinguished from policies, and those which are of only individual concern, or limited scope and duration, as distinguished from those of general consequence and permanent character.

Another interesting distinction respecting "treaties" is made by the Constitution itself. By Article II, Section 2, the exclusive power to make treaties is declared to be in the President and the Senate; by Article I, Section 10, the states are prohibited from entering into any treaty, alliance or confederation; and, by a later provision in the same section the states are prohibited from entering into any agreement or compact with another state, or with a foreign power *without the consent of Congress.* Conversely, it follows by logical inference, a state may enter into *some* agreements or compacts with a foreign power *with* the consent of Congress. Since the exclusive power to make treaties has not only been affirmatively conferred upon the President and the Senate but negatively forbidden to the states, it must result that the international compacts which they may make with the consent of Congress, are not "treaties" within the meaning of the other constitutional provisions. Here again the line of separation between those compacts with foreign powers which may be made, with the consent of Congress, and those which, being "treaties," may not be made by any state under any conditions, has never been drawn, and remains vague and indefinite. So far as I know, there has never been an attempt on the part of a state to make a compact of any kind with a foreign power, and the consent of Congress has never been sought; although there are, of course, numerous instances of agreements and compacts between states which have received the formal consent of Congress. The practical effect of the provision, so far as it concerns agreements and compacts with foreign powers, is restrictive rather than enabling; that is, it operates to put it beyond the power of a state to make any arrangement, however informal, with a foreign government, since Congress is not likely to ever consent to anything which involves official negotiation or intercourse between a state of the Union and a foreign power—the evident and clear purpose of the Constitution being to leave the entire management of our foreign relations to the national government.

The grant of the treaty-making power is so important that it is worth while to have before us the precise language of the Constitution. It is as follows: "The President . . . shall have power, by and with the advice and consent of the Senate, to make treaties, provided two-thirds of the Senators present concur." It will be observed that the advice and consent of the Senate qualifies the power of the President to *make*, not to *negotiate*, treaties. When a treaty is contemplated, therefore, the President may, and more often

does, enter upon negotiations with the foreign government, through diplomatic channels, and carries them
to the point of reaching an understanding as to the
terms and phraseology of the treaty, before the advice
and consent of the Senate is sought at all—subject, of
course, finally, to Senatorial action. But the power of
the Senate, nevertheless, is to advise as well as consent,
and its power is co-ordinate, throughout, with that of
the President. The Senate is not obliged to await the
initiation of the President; it may itself properly take
the first step—and has done so more than once, by
passing a resolution requesting the Chief Executive
to open negotiations with a foreign country, with a
view to concluding a particular treaty. The President
is, of course, strictly within his authority, if he decline
to follow the advice, and, in that case, the Senate can
go no further, since it has no means, if it had the power,
of conducting negotiations on its own account.

The President, upon his part, may, and frequently
does, consult the Senate before initiating negotiations,
or completing negotiations already undertaken, with
a view to obtaining advice in advance. Thus the right
and authority of the Senate to participate in the making of treaties at any stage of the process, has been
again and again recognized and acted upon by the
Executive. Such long continued and uniform action
constitutes a practical construction of the constitutional
provision on the part of those charged with its administration, which the courts would be constrained to follow
should it be possible to present the question in any
justiciable form. It is a matter of history that the
first President met with the Senate upon two or three

occasions in 1789, for the purpose of conferring with, and ascertaining the views of, that body respecting the terms of a treaty in process of negotiation with certain Indian tribes. The matter seems to have been fully discussed between the President and the Senate, and a vote finally taken upon the questions which the President had submitted. While the practice of consulting the Senate in person was not followed by succeeding Presidents, there, nevertheless, have been frequent instances of such consultation by message and by other less formal methods.

It is not an unusual circumstance for the Secretary of State, who is the direct representative of the President in all matters of foreign affairs, to request a confidential conference with the Senate Committee on Foreign Relations, respecting the attitude of the Senate upon some contemplated treaty, or respecting the precise terms which will meet with their approval and support, and with the probable approval and support of the Senate.

The wisdom of the framers of the Constitution in having vested the treaty-making power in the President, with the advice and consent of the Senate, is apparent. In the Convention there was great variety of sentiment on the subject. Upon the one extreme hand, there were those who favored lodging the power with both Houses of Congress, and, upon the other, those who thought it should be vested in the President alone; there were others who suggested the House of Representatives as the appropriate body in whom the power should be reposed; and still others who were in favor of placing it with the Senate alone; and, indeed, the matter was, at one time, disposed of by placing it with the last-named body, and so reported by the Committee of Detail to the Convention. In the end, the plan which was finally adopted commended itself to the good sense of the Convention as insuring preliminary secrecy and expedition whenever necessary, without losing the benefit of the thorough consideration and popular approval, which would result from the independent action of the Senate, in which every state would have an equal vote and an equal opportunity of being heard. Negotiation with foreign governments is a matter of such delicacy that it can be carried on far better by a single person, like the President, than by a large number of officials, like the Senate; while the combined judgment of the larger number—including both President and Senate—respecting the value and wisdom of the result of the negotiation, will generally prove a safer reliance.

The unwisdom of premature and sometimes of ultimate public disclosure of treaty, or other, negotiations with foreign governments, is so clear, that the refusal of President Washington to accede to a request from the House of Representatives to lay before that body the instructions, correspondence and documents relating to the negotiation of the Jay treaty, was approved by the House itself, and has ever since been recognized as establishing a wise precedent for subsequent guidance. President Washington, in his reply, said:

"The nature of foreign negotiations requires caution, and their success must often depend on secrecy; and even when brought to a conclusion a full disclosure of all the measures, demands, or eventual concessions which may have been proposed or contemplated would be extremely impolitic; for this might have a pernicious influence on future negotiations, or produce immediate inconveniences, perhaps, danger and mischief, in relation to other powers. The necessity of such caution and secrecy was one cogent reason for vesting the power of making treaties in the President, with the advice and consent of the Senate, the principle on which that body was formed confining it to a small number of members. To admit, then, a right in the House of Representatives to demand and to have as a matter of course all the papers respecting a negotiation with a foreign power would be to establish a dangerous precedent."

The distinction between foreign affairs and domestic affairs, in the matter of publicity, is recognized by the very form of the requisitions preferred on the part of the respective Houses, for information in the hands of the Executive Departments. When information from the Secretary of the Interior, the Postmaster-General, or any executive head other than the Secretary of State, is desired, the resolution *directs* the officer to furnish it; but in the case of the State Department, dealing with foreign affairs, the resolution *requests* the information "if not incompatible with the public interests." A reply that to furnish the information will not be compatible with the public interests is seldom questioned.

When a treaty has been transmitted to the Senate for its action, the power of that body is plenary. The treaty may be ratified precisely as formulated, amended in any particular deemed advisable, or rejected altogether. The power of the Senate to amend—or, more accurately speaking, to suggest amendments to—a treaty has been sometimes doubted. It has been urged that the power to advise and consent to a treaty must be exercised unconditionally, one way or the other; but the authority of the Senate is not thus categorically limited. The power is not only to consent, or withhold consent, to the making of a treaty, but it is to *advise* and consent. "The President . . . shall have power by and with the *advice* and consent of the Senate to make treaties," is the language of the Constitution. By what warrant may we insert restrictions upon a power thus unconditionally recited? The Senate, by this provision, is constituted a part of the treaty-*making* power, and is authorized to participate in the making as well as to approve or reject. So long as a treaty remains in the Senate unacted upon, it is *in fieri*, that is, not complete but in process of being made, and any advice which is pertinent to the process must obviously be within the power of the Senate to give. To deny this is to ignore the power of the Senate to advise at all—that is to counsel with the President—and to confine that body to functions implied by the word "consent" alone. The Senate has uniformly construed its power in accordance with the view here expressed, having amended scores of treaties since the foundation of the government; and this practical construction has received the approval of the Supreme Court of the United States.[5]

Presidents from the beginning, in one way or in another, as already stated, have freely consulted the Senate with reference to the terms of treaties in process of negotiation. The practice is a good one, and no wise President will fail to follow it upon all advisable occasions. It tends to the maintenance of cordial relations between the two, and enables the President to

[5] 9 Wall. 32–34.

negotiate with more freedom and certainty, because of his knowledge of the attitude of the Senate with respect to the matters involved.

The necessity of having the action of the Senate upon every treaty, however, is not always free from disadvantage. Sometimes haste is essential, and the Senate is a deliberate, as well as a deliberative body. The necessity of debating treaties behind closed doors probably shortens the discussion by the exclusion of the galleries, but, nevertheless, where ninety-six men have the privilege of unlimited discussion, the process is often slow and tedious. Sometimes the necessity of meeting the diverging views of such a number of men results in some sacrifice or apparent sacrifice of national consistency, or in a policy which lacks, or seems to lack, firmness. On the whole, however, the plan provided in the Constitution has the clear balance of advantage.

With the increased participation of our government in foreign affairs, which is sure to follow the conclusion of the present war, the need of close and constant co-operation between the Executive and the Senate will be greatly accentuated. There will, too, be increased need for the service in the Senate of men trained in diplomatic usage and international law, and of broad information about international problems, as well as foresight and tact, without which, mere information may often be of little value.

A question which has been much discussed, and as to which there never has been common agreement, is whether the advice and consent of the Senate may be constitutionally dispensed with in the case of a special

agreement made in pursuance of a general treaty providing for the arbitration of specified controversies between ourselves and a foreign power. In 1905, there
was presented to the Senate by the President a number
of general arbitration treaties which had been negotiated
with France and nine other countries. Article I of
these treaties provided as follows: "Differences which
may arise of a legal nature, or relating to the interpretation of treaties existing between the two contracting
parties, and which it may not have been possible to
settle by diplomacy, shall be referred to the Permanent
Court of Arbitration, established at the Hague by the
Convention of the 29th of July, 1899, provided, nevertheless, that they do not affect the vital interests, the
independence or the honor of the two contracting states,
and do not concern the interests of third parties."
These treaties contained a further provision, set forth
in Article II, which reads: "In each individual case the
high contracting parties, before appealing to the Permanent Court of Arbitration, shall conclude a special
agreement defining clearly the matter in dispute and
the scope of the powers of the arbitrators, and fixing
the periods for the formation of the arbitral tribunal,
and the several stages of the procedure." The provision
in these treaties for a special agreement at once met
with the strong opposition of the Senate. It was insisted that, if incorporated, it would have the effect of
permitting the President to make a special agreement
without the advice and consent of the Senate, and
would therefore constitute a delegation of its treaty-
making power, and that this would be neither constitutional nor wise. It was, therefore, proposed in the

Senate to amend the clause by striking out the word "agreement" and substituting the word "treaty," so as to require a special *treaty* with the advice and consent of the Senate instead of a special *agreement* by the President alone. This position of the Senate the President vigorously combatted, insisting that the provision did not involve a delegation of the treaty-making power, since the "treaty" would already have been made, and the conclusion of any special agreement in pursuance of its terms would simply be in execution of an existing obligation and not the making of a new one. He further insisted that the treaty would lose its principal value if every special agreement made under it should require all the formal steps involved in the consideration and ratification of a treaty under the Constitution. The Senate, however, insisted upon its views and amended the treaties accordingly. The President thereupon signified his determination not to proceed further with the matter, and the treaties were never ratified.

Subsequently, however, in 1908 and 1909, twenty-five general arbitration treaties were negotiated with foreign countries, including all the great powers with the exception of Germany, Russia and Turkey. These treaties which were submitted to the Senate, expressly provided that the special agreement referred to should be made "with the advice and consent of the Senate." In this form they were all approved by the Senate and ratified.

In 1911, under President Taft's administration, two treaties in identical language were negotiated with Great Britain and France, by which certain changes were made in the provisions of the former treaties of

1908. The first clause was somewhat expanded. The differences between the high contracting parties which were to become the subject of arbitration, it was provided, should be those arising "by virtue of a claim of right made by one against the other, under treaty or otherwise, and which are justiciable in their nature by reason of being susceptible of decision by the application of the principles of law or equity." Provision was made for a special agreement of submission in each case which should provide for the organization of the tribunal, if necessary (that is, where some tribunal other than the Permanent Court of Arbitration should be selected), define the scope of the powers of the arbitrators, the question or questions at issue, and settle the terms of reference and the procedure thereunder. No change was made in the provision requiring the special agreement to be made with the advice and consent of the Senate; but an additional provision was incorporated providing that in case of disagreement as to whether a difference was subject to arbitration under Article I, that question should be submitted to a Joint High Commission of Inquiry, and if this Commission, or all but one of its members, should decide that the difference fell within the scope of Article I, it should then be referred to arbitration in accordance with the treaty. The Joint High Commission thus provided for was to be made up of three members selected by each party to the dispute, or in any particular case, according to the terms of the conference; the result of which would be that the Commission would probably—and, in any event, could—in each instance be made up by the selection of three Americans and three citizens or subjects of the other party to the dispute. There was again strenuous objection on the part of the Senate to this provision for the submission to a Commission of the question of the arbitrable character of the dispute, where the high contracting parties did not agree upon it; and it was again insisted that such a provision involved a delegation of the treaty-making power. The result was that this provision was stricken from the treaties before their approval. The action of the Senate was, apparently, based upon the report of the Committee on Foreign Relations to the effect that to "take away from the Senate the determination of the most important question in a proposed treaty of arbitration is necessarily in violation of the treaty provisions of the Constitution. The most vital question in every proposed arbitration is whether the difference is arbitrable." With the utmost respect for the opinions of those senators who constitute a majority, I have never been able to agree with their conclusion, and I think the action of the Senate constituted a distinct impairment of the value of the treaties.

The conclusion that the provision in question constituted a delegation of the treaty-making power seems to me wholly without warrant. The treaties laid down a general rule by which the arbitrable character of the differences was to be determined. That rule was that the differences should (1) arise by virtue of a claim of right made by one against the other under treaty or otherwise, and (2) that it should be justiciable in its nature by reason of being susceptible of decision by the application of the principles of law or equity. This furnishes a definite standard by reference to which the question is to be determined. That it might sometimes be a difficult question to determine, does not alter the fact that the treaty furnishes the standard. It is frequently the case with statutes that even persons skilled in the elucidation of their mysteries may differ as to their meaning and application in given cases. In any such case, if the parties concerned and their legal advisers are unable to finally agree, the remedy is to present the question to a court, which acts as an umpire to decide who is right. Nobody will, of course, pretend that such a process involves a delegation of the law-making power. The law-making function has already acted and what follows is the operation of the law-interpreting function. An exactly parallel situation was presented by the treaty provision in question. When the general arbitration treaty was made and ratified the treaty-making process was complete. To determine whether or not a given case fell within or fell without the terms of the treaty, as already recited, involved not the treaty-making function but the treaty-construing function. There was no attempt to delegate a power to make a treaty covering the special case as it arose; but an authority was conferred to determine whether the facts of the given case came within the broad but definite jurisdictional provisions of a general treaty already made. The determination of such a question by the Joint High Commission would be no more the exercise of the treaty-making power than the determination by a judge that a complaint states a case under a general statute, and that the court has jurisdiction to consider and decide it, would be the exercise of the law-making power. In addition to this, the special agreement provided for would, under the treaty, still go to the Senate for its advice and consent, should the Commission decide the differences to be arbitrable, precisely as in the case where the high contracting parties so decide in the first instance. In either event the Senate would have the final word. The action of the Senate, therefore, presented the obvious inconsistency of maintaining that the authority conferred upon the Commission to determine the preliminary jurisdictional question constituted a delegation of the treaty power of the Senate, while the same authority conferred upon the high contracting parties did not. The provision for the Commission would have had a tendency to increase the utilization of the process of arbitration since it would have kept the door of opportunity open after the negative determination of the high contracting parties, the value of which is apparent; but the final authority of the Senate would have remained precisely the same.

The practical objections that were made, namely, that we might be compelled to arbitrate such questions as the Monroe Doctrine or the right to exclude aliens, or other purely American questions, were to my mind equally without foundation. Such questions cannot be said to be justiciable or susceptible of decision by the application of the principles of law or equity. These questions constitute political policies, and would no more come within the scope of the powers of arbitration, as laid down by this treaty, than the question of whether an individual is justified in declining to be on visiting terms with some neighbor would constitute a proper subject for judicial inquiry.

In addition to this, the consent of at least two out of three of our own citizens, who would be members of the Commission, would be required before any such question could be held justiciable, and the chance, therefore, of its ever being thus determined, was so remote as to be practically impossible. Nations, as well as individuals, have rights which by their very nature are insusceptible of submission to the determination of any tribunal; as, for example, the right of an individual to his own opinions or to choose his own associates, and, as for example, the right of a nation to select its own political principles and policies, form of government, and determine who may and who may not be admitted to its territory or partake of its citizenship.

The fear that was expressed by some to the effect that under the terms of the treaty we might be obliged to arbitrate matters affecting the national honor was equally ill founded. National honor, and personal honor as well, are very real and precious things to be preserved at even great hazard, whenever actually assailed; but "honor" is a flexible and much-abused term, the meaning and application of which, all too frequently, depends upon an artificial point of view, and is narrowed or broadened by temperamental and racial differences, or by the sentimental influences of the moment. It is a melancholy fact that a good deal that is utterly spurious passes current under the name of "honor." History is replete with instances where in the first heat of resentment one nation has regarded its honor as having been assailed by another, only to conclude after a period of reflection that an over-sensitive view of the matter had been taken. The question of "honor" is so often and so greatly influenced by the personal equation that if made a formal basis of action, or a formal limitation upon action, it is sure, sooner or later, to result in a situation where the distinction between genuine sentiment and fictitious sentimentality will disappear. We know that when the duello was the recognized remedy for wounded self-esteem mere matters of punctilio were frequently exaggerated into affairs of honor. There may some day, of course, arise that rare and exceptional case when the affront to the national honor will be so unquestionable and so grave that the indignation of the people, even after reflection, would sweep aside every restraint that stands in the way of the swift punishment of the aggressor; but it is difficult to conceive any such case as falling within the description of "differences . . . susceptible of decision by the application of the principles of law or equity;" and I do not imagine that any American member of a Joint High Commission would ever so decide. On the other hand, whenever the case for one side or the other is without merit, the presence in a treaty of an exception so equivocal will afford an altogether too convenient pretext upon which to base a refusal to submit a perfectly legitimate controversy to arbitration. These two treaties have never been ratified, and it is unfortunate that such dubious phrases as "vital interests" and "honor of the contracting states" remain as exceptions in existing treaties. As said by former Secretary, now Senator, Knox: "These are terms of wide and varied general meaning, which are not judicially definable and mean whatever the particular nation involved declares them to mean."

Article VI of the Constitution declares that treaties made, or which shall be made, under the authority of the United States, shall be the supreme law of the land in common with the Constitution itself and all laws of the United States made in pursuance of the Constitution. This provision has introduced into our political system an interesting principle of far-reaching importance. A treaty, primarily and in all its international aspects, is simply a contract between two or more sovereign parties. It does not ordinarily constitute international law although it is frequently valuable as evidence tending to establish what that law is in some disputed particular. There are, to be sure, certain treaties, signed by substantially all the civilized nations, of such recognized authority that the principles they announce have come to be accepted as rules of international law; but even these treaties may be regarded not as constituting substantive international law, but rather as evidence of the law of such a conclusive character as to foreclose further question. International law is law of the land, and courts take judicial notice of it as they do of domestic law. That is true of Great Britain and was true before the separation of the Colonies, and it has always been a recognized principle of our own jurisprudence. But a treaty is not primarily law of the land. However conclusive its provisions, it is essentially an agreement which does not operate of its own force to accomplish the objects set forth. Under the constitutional provision, however, a treaty is not only a contract but it is law, with the result that whenever it *establishes* rights as distinguished from *promising* them, it has the effect of an act of legislation to be enforced by the courts. Where, however, the treaty is executory, and requires some action to effectuate its provisions, as for example an appropriation of money by Congress, it is subject not to the judicial but to the political power. An executory treaty, requiring further legislation or executive action, is obviously not a law any more than a bill is a law, which has passed one House and not the other, or has passed both Houses but lacks the approval of the President. In other words, such a treaty cannot be law of the land because, while it is complete as a contract, it is not complete as a law, and does not become complete until it has been supplemented by the requisite political action. When this has been taken, any justiciable right established by the treaty plus the supplemental action, will become subject to judicial enforcement. It follows that the provision making a treaty the supreme law of the land is not to be interpreted literally, but, so far as the judicial power of the courts is concerned, includes only such treaties as are self-executing. So long as the concurrence of Congress is required, or some further action of the Executive is necessary, to render the treaty operative, it does not reach the dignity of law.

It will be seen that laws made in pursuance of the Constitution, as well as treaties made under the authority of the United States, shall be the supreme law, and there is nothing in the language of the provision or elsewhere in the Constitution to indicate that either is of superior efficacy to the other. The result is, as the Supreme Court has decided, that either may be superseded by the other. A treaty may have the effect of repealing an Act of Congress, or an Act of Congress of repealing a treaty.[6]

Thus, the legislation of Congress excluding Chinese immigrants, which utterly contravened certain provisions of a Chinese treaty, was held to effect a repeal or a modification of these provisions, and was binding upon the courts.[7]

If Congress, by legislation, may annul a treaty which is self-executing and, therefore, law, it may likewise repeal or alter legislation passed to make the treaty effective, or refuse to enact such legislation in the first instance; and in either event the courts are without power to interfere in any way. A party to the treaty has no redress except to appeal to the moral sense of the other party, and that failing, to either submit or declare war. It is needless, however, to say that Congress cannot by abrogating a treaty disturb property rights which have already become vested in pursuance of its terms.

The power of Congress to abrogate a treaty or to refuse to enact legislation necessary to effectuate a treaty or to repeal or alter such legislation after its enactment, should be exercised only for the clearest and most compelling reasons—reasons which will rarely exist outside the justifying principles of international law. Mere hardship, however severe, the presence in the treaty of unwise stipulations, even to the point of folly, will never justify its exercise; for these are considerations which, it must be conclusively assumed, were weighed

[6] 11 Wall 620.
[7] 130 U. S. 581.

by the makers of the treaty by whose determination we become irrevocably bound. Nations like individuals must stand by their bargains, whether they turn out to be profitable and wise, or burdensome and foolish. In no other way and upon no other principle can international intercourse be decently maintained. The very fact that the affirmative action of Congress in these respects cannot be judicially or otherwise authoritatively reviewed and set aside, if wrong—nor the failure of Congress to act, when failure is inexcusable, become the basis of coercive measures—emphasizes the necessity for the most exact observance of the obligations which the duly constituted treaty-making agencies of the government have assumed. The word of honor of a nation, like the word of honor of a man, once given, passes into the realm of undebatable things. That a treaty is only "a scrap of paper" is a doctrine so depraved that any nation which gives it sanction deserves to be held for all time in the just scorn of all faith-keeping peoples.

CHAPTER VII

THE TREATY-MAKING POWER— HOW FAR LIMITED

One of the most important questions connected with the subject of treaty-making is that which concerns the extent of the power, the discussion of which will now be undertaken. Is this power plenary or limited? If the latter, how and by what authority is it limited and what are the limitations? The first question is susceptible of a ready answer; the second is one of difficulty.

The power is subject to limitations imposed both by international law and by the terms and implications of the Constitution. The limitations of the first class arise from certain fundamental principles of the law of nations essentially analogous to what is called in municipal law "public policy." The freedom of international contract is limited by these principles as the freedom of private contract is limited by this policy. And precisely as public policy is more or less elastic, these principles are more or less elastic, and expand and contract in response to the prevailing opinions of the times. There is, of course, no requirement that the high contracting parties in making their agreements shall stipulate for the recognition of rights or the enforcement of obligations in conformity with any positive rules of the law of nations. They are at liberty to make such engagements as they choose, whether the rights declared or the obligations assumed accord with, or differ from, those which would be enforced by the law of nations in the absence of agreement, provided these principles are not infringed; just as individuals may assume obligations entirely different in character or degree from those which would, in the absence of agreement, be imposed by the positive rules of the municipal law, provided their stipulations are not contrary to public policy. All this, of course, is quite obvious.

It has sometimes been said that the term "law" is not applicable to the rules which govern the intercourse of nations, since these rules have neither the command nor the coercive power of a supreme authority behind them. The term is, nevertheless, substantially accurate, for these rules, while not ordered nor enforced by a superior authority, are rules of action in their nature obligatory rather than advisory, which nations are constrained to respect and follow under the compelling pressure of the opinions of civilized mankind. It is true, in one sense, that nations may make with one another such contracts as they please, but, nevertheless, certain stipulations which are opposed to international principles and policies are unlawful. A treaty may not require the doing of something undeniably contrary to morality or justice. Thus, a treaty requiring one of the contracting parties, without cause, to break a treaty obligation due to a third party would be clearly obnoxious to the plainest principles of international morality, and it is impossible to concede that the authority to make such a treaty is within the legitimate power of any treaty-making agency. The same would be true of a treaty which undertook to re-establish the slave trade; to control the use of the sea, that common international highway; or to invade and subjugate another independent and unoffending nation.

We are, however, more especially concerned with the limitations imposed by the Constitution or by the nature of our own institutions. Certain limitations are effected by positive prohibitions. Whatever the Constitution forbids absolutely, of course, may not be done by a treaty any more than by any other method. No such restrictions are imposed upon the treaty-making power, however, in specific terms, as in the case of the law-making powers. Moreover, the treaty-making power is conferred in general terms, while the subjects with which the law-making power may deal are carefully enumerated, which, in itself, constitutes a limitation, in consonance with the rule that the expression of one thing excludes other things. A sufficient reason for this enumeration in the case of the law-making powers and the absence of it in the case of the treaty-making power, lies in the fact that the former are divided between the states and the Nation, while the latter is confined exclusively to the Nation. These differences are typical of the exclusive as well as the broad character of the external powers of the national government generally.

No limitations upon the treaty-making power, therefore, exist by reason of the terms in which the power is conferred, or by reason of any *directly* restrictive language; but such as do exist result "from the nature and fundamental principles of our government" which forbid that a treaty should "change the Constitution or be held valid if it be in violation of that instrument." [1]

[1] 11 Wall 620.

It is needless to say that such limitations are restrictive only upon our own governmental agencies. Necessarily they are not controlling upon other nations since the Constitution has no extraterritorial operation. Theoretically, the United States might be bound by the obligations of a treaty under the law of nations, from which it would be absolved under the Constitution. Since, however, foreign governments in dealing with us must look into the Constitution sufficiently, at least, to see what political agencies have the treaty-making power, it is not without reason to maintain that they will also be bound to take notice of the limitations upon the authority of these agencies, in analogy to a similar principle in the law of agency which denies the liability of the principal for his agent's acts, beyond the known or apparent scope of the latter's authority. However this may be, and whatever the case may be in respect of treaties regarded as international obligations, it is certain that considered from the standpoint of municipal law, they may not contravene the applicable restraints of the Constitution, or such restraints as arise from the nature of the government instituted by the Constitution. In other words, while the treaty-making power is conferred without any express reservations it is, nevertheless, subject to certain fundamental limitations. Mr. Justice Field described these limitations generally as precluding the treaty-making power from authorizing "what the Constitution forbids, or a change in the character of the government or in that of one of the states, or a cession of any portion of the territory of the latter without its consent." Beyond these exceptions, he says, the power may be exercised respecting any matter properly the subject of negotiations with a foreign country.[2]

Mr. Calhoun in his "Discourse on the Constitution and Government of the United States" enumerates the limitations in more detail. What he says may be briefly epitomized as follows:

1. The questions dealt with must be *inter alios*, that is, questions between the United States and foreign powers requiring adjustment.

2. The power is limited by all the provisions of the Constitution which inhibit certain acts, or which direct acts to be done in a particular way.

3. It is not competent (*a*) to change the character of the government or (*b*) to do that which can be done only by the constitution-making power, or (*c*) to do that which is inconsistent with the nature and structure of the government or the objects for which it was formed, among which is included the lack of power to change or alter the boundary of a state or cede any part of its territory without its consent.

Let us examine these suggestions seriatum:

1. That the power extends only to questions between the parties requiring adjustment is a practical if it were not a legal limitation, since it is not to be supposed that nations will care to negotiate and make treaties respecting affairs by which they are not mutually affected; and their own determination of the matter should ordinarily control. If, however, a treaty should be concluded with the United States, for example, making disposition of exclusively internal affairs, undoubtedly it would be invalid, as an attempt to deal with matters not the subject of treaty with a foreign

[2] 133 U. S. 266.

power. Such a treaty would be either a specious subterfuge or an intolerable and inadmissible interference on the part of another nation with our domestic concerns.

2. It is clear that when the Constitution prohibits absolutely the doing of any particular act, it is but an illustration of the prohibition to say that the act cannot be done under the power to make treaties; and it is equally clear that when the Constitution directs that an act shall be done only in a particular way, it may not be stipulated for in a treaty if that involve the doing of it in another and different way; as, for example, an appropriation of money from the Treasury, since the Constitution provides that "no money shall be drawn from the Treasury but in consequence of appropriations made by law." However, a treaty stipulation for the payment of money, although requiring Congressional action, will ordinarily constitute a moral obligation upon Congress to enact the necessary legislation. Such a treaty is *obligatory* though not *effective*. It is seldom that a treaty requires any further action on the part of the contracting governments to render it obligatory, but there are occasional instances where the promise is to advise or recommend legislative action instead of promising performance of the act, in which case the treaty is neither obligatory nor effective until the requisite legislation has been enacted.

3. Clearly it would not be competent by treaty to change the form of government or usurp functions of the Constitution-making power or alter the nature or structure of the government, or the objects for which it was formed. And this for the double reason that such action would not only violate the Constitution or the funda-

mental principles upon which it rests, but also because it would constitute a gratuitous intrusion upon the purely internal affairs of the Nation; therefore, a subject outside the scope of international negotiation and agreement.

The illustration which Mr. Calhoun gives under this head, however, constitutes a case lying outside the principle rather than an example of it. It must, therefore, receive separate consideration. To change or alter the boundary of a state or cede a part of its territory without its consent, does not change the form of government, nor do that which can only be done by the Constitution-making power, nor is it inconsistent with the nature or structure of the government or the objects for which it was formed. If such action be outside the treaty-making power of the national government it must be for reasons quite apart from any of these considerations. There is nothing in the Constitution which specifically prohibits such a treaty. The form, nature and structure of the government is a matter of organization, not a matter of geography; the Constitution-making power has to do with the original form and the subsequent amendment of the Constitution; and the objects of the government are those set forth in the preamble and the substantive provisions of the Constitution, and nowhere include the preservation of the geographical integrity of the states as one of these objects. The obligations of the United States to the several states, so far as they are set forth, are to guarantee to each a republican form of government, and to protect each against invasion and, on application, against domestic violence. The prohibitions against interference with the states are that no state shall be deprived of its equal suffrage in the Senate, that no new state shall be formed within the jurisdiction of another state, nor by the junction of two or more states or parts of states without the consent of the legislatures of the states concerned, and of Congress. There is no prohibition against the cession of state territory. The only question, therefore, is whether such action is precluded by any fundamental implication. The opinion of Mr. Justice Field, already quoted, is entitled to the greatest possible weight, and if there were no opposing authority or countervailing reason, might well be accepted as final.

It is to be observed, in the first place, that the power of a sovereign nation to cede territory lying within its limits and jurisdiction is one which is well recognized by the law of nations, and has been exercised from time immemorial. Alteration of boundaries by cession or otherwise, is one of the normal and usual results of war. The greater part of our own territory—and if we include Indian lands, nearly all of it—has been acquired by negotiated cession or enforced as a result of conquest. The power of the treaty-making agencies with whom we dealt must, of course, be affirmed, since to deny it is to impeach our own title to the ceded lands. As the result of the Mexican War we exacted the treaty of Guadaloupe Hidalgo, by which the cession of a tract of country of imperial extent was made, and since erected into states of the Union. The following question, therefore, is pertinent, and not to be easily answered in the negative: Suppose Mexico, instead of being weak had been powerful, and that she, instead of ourselves, had been successful, and after invading

Texas, then a state in the Union but quite recently theretofore Mexican territory, had demanded as the price of peace the cession of the whole or a part of this former possession—could the national government, without the consent of the state of Texas, have made the cession in order to terminate the war and save other and additional territory from invasion and conquest? Is any other than an affirmative answer, under these circumstances, possible? If not, it follows that the national government when the necessity is supreme has the power to cede territory without the consent of the state in which it lies. And, of course, the treaty-making power of the Nation must be the judge of that necessity.

Mr. Jefferson was of the opinion that the General government did not possess the power. Mr. Hamilton was of the contrary opinion, and Mr. Jefferson conceded that as the "result of a disastrous war the abandonment of territory might be necessary." [3]

Mr. Justice Story, replying to an inquiry of Edward Everett in 1838, gave it as his opinion that such a cession might be made where it was indispensable to purchase peace, or calculated to promote the safety of both nations, or constituted an equivalent for a cession by the other side, and therefore it could not be admitted to be universally true that the power did not exist. [4]

Chancellor Kent, according to Professor Woolsey, was of opinion that this power of cession belonged exclusively to the United States, though as a matter of sound discretion the assent of the state governments

[3] 5 Moore, International Law, 172.
[4] *Ibid.*, 173.

should be obtained.[5] And Professor Woolsey, while evidently reluctant to concede the power, says: "Only in extreme cases where the treaty-making power is called upon to accept the *fact* of conquest, or to save the whole body from ruin by surrendering a part, could such an exercise of power be justified." [6]

Mr. Butler, after reviewing the whole subject, emphatically affirms the authority of the general government.[7] That the power exists, subject to some ill-defined limitations respecting the necessity of its exercise in given cases, I think is a logical and necessary conclusion.

May the treaty-making power, without the concurrence of Congress, lawfully dispose of a matter which, by the Constitution, is committed to the jurisdiction of that body? We have seen that an attempt by treaty to appropriate money from the Treasury would not be operative; but this does not quite answer the question, since that may result not from the fact that the affirmative power to appropriate money belongs to Congress but from the fact that the Constitution clearly requires that no money shall be drawn from the Treasury in any other way. But the mere fact that Congress is authorized to legislate upon a particular subject does not, in my judgment, remove it from the jurisdiction of the treaty-making power, nor prevent treaty stipulations respecting it from becoming obligatory and effective without Congressional action. A conclusion to that extent would seem to be involved in the consideration

[5] 1 Butler, Treaty-Making Power, 413.
[6] 2 Butler, 393.
[7] 2 Butler, 393, 394.

that a treaty duly concluded by the constitutional agencies may have the effect of repealing a prior act of Congress. Such a treaty necessarily disposes of a matter within the enumerated powers of Congress since it repeals a statute passed in pursuance of these powers. That a treaty, by its terms self-executing, may have this effect has been decided by the Supreme Court more than once, and is no longer open to question. From the beginning, however, the House of Representatives has consistently maintained that while it constitutes no part of the treaty-making agency of the Nation, nevertheless, a treaty which undertakes to dispose of a subject included within the law-making powers of Congress is inoperative until it has received the approval of Congress, a proposition which has generally, though not uniformly, been denied by the Senate, and which also seems quite clearly to be denied by the Supreme Court. Mr. Justice Field, in one of the Chinese exclusion cases, said:

"If the treaty relates to *a subject within the powers of Congress* and operates by its own force, it can only be regarded by the courts as equivalent to a legislative act." [8]

Mr. Justice Gray held that the admission of aliens might be forbidden or regulated either by means of a treaty, or by an act of Congress passed under the power to regulate foreign commerce, and other powers enumerated in the Constitution.[9] The fact is that numerous treaties regulating foreign commerce, self-operative by their terms, have been enforced without congressional

[8] 112 U. S. 562.
[9] 142 U. S. 649.

legislation, and upheld as law of the land by the courts. Upon that subject, Mr. Justice Field said:

"The right or privilege being conferred by the treaty, parties seeking to enjoy it take whatever steps are necessary to carry the provisions into effect. Those who wish to engage in commerce enter our ports with their ships and cargoes; those who wish to reside here select their places of residence, *no congressional legislation being required to provide that they shall enjoy the rights and privileges stipulated.*" [10]

In this connection it may again be observed, that the power to make treaties is conferred upon the President and the Senate without reservation or exception of any kind—two-thirds of the Senators present concurring in the approval in order to make the treaty effectual. To procure such a vote of the Senate will generally be not less difficult than to procure a bare majority of each House; and the Framers evidently believed that the participation of the Senate, with this requirement of a two-thirds vote, would constitute a sufficient safeguard in all cases. The matter of having the action of the House, as well as the Senate, was not overlooked but received careful consideration and was deliberately rejected. In view of these facts it is difficult to escape the conclusion that it was the clear intention of the Framers to make the action of the President and Senate conclusive *in all cases;* and to give to all self-executing treaties the force of law without the concurrence of Congress as a whole, whether these treaties disposed of subjects enumerated among the law-making powers or not. If an exception in favor of the subjects committed to Congress had been intended, the failure to

[10] 120 U. S. 704.

provide for it in precise terms is inexplicable, and the absence of it is strongly persuasive evidence that no such exception was intended or is admissable. The position of the House is now, however, generally followed in practice, and the question has become more or less academic in view of the fact that the House has never refused, and is not likely to refuse, to join with the Senate in passing any legislation thought necessary to carry into effect or affirm treaty obligations. Nevertheless, and while there is among students of the subject opinion to the contrary, I have no doubt that the specific delegation of certain powers to Congress in no manner limits or qualifies the authority of the treaty-making agencies to deal with the same subjects except in those cases where some particular power is made exclusive by the terms or implications of the Constitution, or is rendered so as a necessary result of the intrinsic nature of the power itself.

The necessity of supplementary action to carry into operation treaty provisions which are not made self-executing, has the effect of authorizing Congress to legislate upon many matters which would be beyond its power in the absence of a treaty. In such case the authority is not derived from, nor is it limited by, the enumerated subjects of legislation; but it arises from that clause of the Constitution which empowers Congress "to make all laws which shall be necessary and proper for carrying into execution the foregoing powers, and all other powers vested by this Constitution in the government of the United States, or in any department, or officer thereof." The power exercised in any such case is as strictly constitutional as in the case of the specifically enumerated powers, but occasion for legislative action in this field has no limits except those which bound the treaty-making power itself. The treaty-making power being one of those "vested by the Constitution in the government of the United States," the authority of Congress to pass all laws to carry it into execution is conferred by the co-efficient clause in precise and definite words.

A striking example of the exercise of this power is afforded by the treaty recently concluded between ourselves and Great Britain for the protection of migratory birds. By the terms of this treaty closed seasons are provided for various sorts of birds within the United States and the Dominion of Canada; and the contracting parties mutually bind themselves to take, or propose to their respective law-making bodies, necessary measures for insuring the execution of the treaty. In pursuance of this, Congress on July 3 of the present year (1918) passed an act to give effect to the treaty, and, among other provisions, devolved upon the Secretary of Agriculture, with the approval of the President, the authority to make regulations in detail to carry out the general provisions of the treaty. Any violation of the treaty, or the act of Congress, or the regulations, is made an offense punishable by fine and imprisonment. In the absence of the treaty it is clear that the subject is one beyond the powers of Congress, since wild game is not the property of the Nation but of the states in their public capacity for the common benefit of their people. Indeed, an act of Congress dealing with the subject in a similar way before the conclusion of the treaty, was held to be unconstitutional.[11] The subject, however, is one in which the two countries are mutually interested, and the evils which the treaty seeks to suppress are of common concern. Hence the matter is one which quite evidently falls within the treaty-making power, and the act of Congress comes within the grant of the co-efficient clause as a law "necessary and proper for carrying into execution . . . powers vested . . . in the government of the United States."

No theory has been more earnestly debated nor has given rise to more pronounced differences of opinion, than that which challenges the validity of a treaty stipulation disposing of a matter which otherwise would fall within the reserved powers of the states; and especially which would fall within their police powers. In the first place, it is necessary to carefully distinguish this proposition from another, already adverted to, with which it is likely to be confused, namely, that the treaty-making power is incompetent to deal with questions exclusively domestic. The difference between the two is apparent: the latter is based upon the doctrine that such questions are not proper subjects for treaties under any circumstances; the former upon the theory that while the given treaty deals with matters within the general scope of the treaty-making power, they are nevertheless questions withheld from the United States and reserved to the states exclusively. It is clear that a treaty, in order to be valid, must have a legitimate international reason as its basis; it can never be made the medium for *meddling* with the purely internal affairs of one of the contracting nations. But assuming

[11] 221 Fed. 288.

this international reason, may a treaty lawfully stipulate for rights or privileges which but for the treaty would confessedly be exclusively under the control of the state? Let me repeat, because it is important in this connection, that the treaty-making power was never possessed or exercised by the states separately; but was originally acquired and always exclusively held by the Nation, and, therefore, could not have been among those carved from the mass of state powers, and handed over to the Nation. But the Constitution is not content with merely confirming this power to the Nation; it goes further and expressly prohibits it to the states. It is, therefore, certain that whatever else may be reserved to the states by the Tenth Amendment, no part of the treaty-making power can possibly be included. Necessarily, then, as the power can be exercised only by the national government, and its denial to that government in any particular is equivalent to forbidding its exercise in that respect altogether, we are forced by all logical rules of construction to conclude that the full power is vested in that government except as limited by the prohibitions of the Constitution, by the character of the government instituted, or by the nature of the power itself. Former Senator Root has stated the matter so clearly and conclusively that I borrow and adopt his words. He said:

"Legislative power is distributed: upon some subjects the national legislature has authority, upon other subjects the state legislature has authority. Judicial power is distributed: in some cases the federal courts have jurisdiction, in other cases the state courts have jurisdiction. Executive power is distributed: in some fields the national executive is to act, in other fields the state executive is to act. The treaty-making power is not distributed; it is all vested in the National government; no part of it is vested in or reserved to the states. In international affairs there are no states; there is but one nation, acting in direct relation and representation of every citizen in every state. Every treaty made under the authority of the United States is made by the National government as the direct and sole representative of every citizen of the United States residing in California equally with every citizen of the United States residing elsewhere. It is, of course, conceivable that, under pretense of exercising the treaty-making power, the President and Senate might attempt to make provisions regarding matters which are not proper subjects of international agreement, and which would be only a colorable—not a real—exercise of the treaty-making power; but so far as the real exercise of the power goes there can be no question of state rights, because the Constitution itself, in the most explicit terms, has precluded the existence of any such question."

When we come to consider that the treaty power is of this essentially exclusive character, that its full exercise necessarily devolves upon the general government as the only possible agency, and that in its legitimate exercise the certainty of an occasional collision with state affairs must have been foreseen, the claim for the supremacy of the police powers of the state must be disallowed, unless we are willing to charge the framers of the Constitution with the folly of conferring a power so incompletely that its exercise in many important and, perhaps, in some vital, particulars may be precluded altogether. The matter is, after all, quite simple, and resolves itself into the question whether the positive provisions of Article VI of the Constitution mean what they seem to say? By this article treaties made under the authority of the United States are declared to be the supreme law of the land, *"anything in the Constitution or laws of any state to the contrary notwithstanding."*

Laws of the United States made in pursuance of the Constitution and treaties made under the authority of the United States stand upon the same footing of equality. The Constitution and laws of the states are expressly made subordinate to both. No language could be more definite or final, and the conclusion is inevitable that a treaty, otherwise valid under the Constitution, is not rendered invalid because it conflicts with some provision of a state constitution or state law. In such case, the repugnancy being shown, both cannot stand; and Article VI solves the question of priority by declaring the supremacy of the treaty.

If it be necessary to have confirmation of the self evident, it may be borne in mind that one of the prime reasons for the incorporation of Article VI in the Constitution, so far as it applies to treaties, was that, under the Confederation, treaties had been notoriously disregarded by the states, and state laws conflicting with treaty stipulations granting individual rights and privileges had been enforced by the state governments. The treaty of 1783 by which peace was made with Great Britain was thus openly and flagrantly defied. That treaty provided that the loyalists whose property had been confiscated under state laws should be compensated for their losses; that impediments to the collection of debts due to British subjects should be removed; and debts paid in the equivalent of British money. Notwithstanding these solemn engagements on the part of the Nation, some of the states passed laws which, in effect, nullified them. As a consequence, the British declined to surrender certain forts which they had agreed to surrender. The Congress of the Confederation passed resolutions declaring that state legislatures had no power to enact laws construing treaties or restraining or controlling their operation, or execution, and declaring that such treaties constituted a part of the law of the land, and as such were binding upon the state legislatures.

This condition of affairs, which the Confederation was utterly powerless to remedy, was the occasion of apprehensive solicitude everywhere among thoughtful men. To permit it to continue was to sap the sovereignty of the Nation and render it contemptible in the sight of all other nations. The anomaly of a sovereignty with power to promise but none to perform could not endure. Either the treaty-making power of the Nation must be made supreme in fact as well as in theory, or the complete supremacy of the states and the disintegration of the Union be allowed to supervene. A division of authority in a matter where singleness of authority was vital had become intolerable and impossible. The power to make treaties, like the power to wage war, was something which the Nation must possess beyond the peradventure of state interference. The intention of the Framers to so provide cannot be doubted, since a necessity so pressing could not be put aside. They began by reaffirming the power to the Nation and made assurance doubly sure by denying it to the states. And then, to remove all possibility of state interference through the exercise of any conceivable state power, they declared that treaties should be the supreme law of the land "*anything* in the Constitution or laws of any state to the contrary notwithstanding." In the face of this imperative language, to insist that a treaty otherwise valid is nevertheless subject to the controlling force of a law passed in pursuance of the police powers of a state, is to blot out the words *"anything* notwithstanding" and substitute *"nearly* anything notwithstanding," and to convert that which is declared without reservation to be supreme into something subject and subordinate.

That the supremacy clause was absolute was clearly the opinion of those who framed it, and those who participated in its adoption. Thus, James Wilson, in the Pennsylvania Ratifying Convention, after calling attention to the repeated violations of the British treaty by the passage of counteracting state legislation, declared that this clause would show the world that we secure the performance of treaties no longer nominally but effectively, "let the legislatures of the different states do what they may." [12] And Mr. Madison in the Virginia Convention, asserting the supremacy of a treaty over state laws, said: "If it does not supersede their existing laws, as far as they contravene its operation, it cannot be of any effect. To counteract it, by the supremacy of the state laws, would bring on the Union the just charge of national perfidy, and involve us in war." [13]

The decisions of the Supreme Court are in clear support of the view here contended for. Mr. Justice Chase in Ware *vs.* Hylton, decided in 1796, said: "A treaty cannot be the supreme law of the land, that is of all the United States, if any act of a state legislature can stand in its way." State laws and Constitutions contrary to the treaty of 1783, then under consideration,

[12] 2 Elliott's Debates, 489–90.
[13] 3 Elliott, 515.

were, by virtue of the supremacy clause, he graphically declared, "prostrated before the treaty." A comprehensive review of the cases which followed would extend this discussion quite beyond the limits I am obliged to observe, and it is, moreover, unnecessary since that service has already been fully performed by Mr. Butler in his scholarly work on the "Treaty-Making Power," and by Professor Corwin in his brilliantly convincing book entitled "National Supremacy."

The most elaborate as well as the ablest presentation of the opposing view of the question, is that contained in the recent work of Henry St. George Tucker—"Limitations on the Treaty-Making Power." Mr. Tucker, as a result of his own analysis and a review of the authorities, concludes (p. 339) that, "no essential power of a state, whether a reserved power or a police power, can by reasonable construction be constitutionally taken from it, in furtherance of the treaty-making power."

Now, in one sense, it is quite correct to say that no essential power can be taken from a state in furtherance of the treaty-making power. A treaty stipulation to the effect that the states should no longer have the power to enact laws to safeguard the public health, for example, would be utterly void, just as an act of Congress so providing would be utterly void; but a state statute enacted *under this police power*, which conflicts with a treaty provision on the same subject, concededly valid in other respects, must yield to the supremacy of the treaty, just as it must in similar circumstances yield to the supremacy of an act of Congress passed in pursuance, let us say, of the authority to regulate commerce. In the latter case, it would be no answer to the claim of supremacy, as the Supreme Court has held, to assert that the statute was enacted under the police power, for, as the court proceeded to say: "It is clear from the nature of our complex form of government, that whenever the statute of a state invades the domain of legislation which belongs exclusively to the Congress of the United States it is void, no matter under what class of powers it may fall, or how clearly allied to powers conceded to belong to the states." [14] That this is also true in the case of treaties which are equally the supreme law, was clearly the opinion of Chief Justice Marshall, who said: "In every such case the act of Congress *or the treaty* is supreme, and the laws of the state, though enacted in the exercise of powers not controverted must yield to it." [15] The powers reserved to the states are not reserved *against* the powers of the United States, but in harmony with and *in subordination to* every such power. The Tenth Amendment read in connection with the supremacy clause can mean nothing else.

The conclusion to which we have come is of great practical importance, for if the claim of supremacy for state police power over treaties be conceded, we are certain, sooner or later, to become involved in conflict, as we have already been in controversy with other nations. The contention over the exclusion of the Japanese from the public schools in California and later over the land question are still fresh in our minds. Only the exercise of great tact, forbearance and patience on the part of the responsible officials of both countries,

[14] 92 U. S. 259.
[15] Gibbons *vs*. Ogden, 9 Wheat 210.

prevented an embarrassing situation from becoming dangerously critical. Whether the proper construction of the treaty involved would justify the claims of the Japanese government or those of California is fairly open to question; but that the treaty-making power of the United States is competent to accord the privileges which were claimed for the subjects of Japan is not, in my judgment, open to legitimate dispute. Not only is it clear that state constitutions and state laws, of whatsoever character, must yield in case of conflict; but an opposite conclusion would be gravely unfortunate, since it would place it in the power of a state to over-ride and confound the national will in matters where the opportunities of the national authorities for accurate and dependable determinations are far better than those of the state authorities, who, not realizing the delicacy of the questions involved, might bring the Nation to the verge of war in an effort to uphold the policies of a single state. The story of the conditions in this respect under the Confederation constitutes a warning which we can never afford to disregard.

That there should ever have been any doubt as to the complete supremacy of the national power in all matters of foreign relation is an anomaly that, under the new and enlarged world responsibilities we are assuming, is no longer tolerable. The eyes of foreign governments see only the Nation. State boundaries are as meaningless to them as county boundaries in Great Britain are to us. In Chisholm vs. Georgia, Mr. Justice Wilson said: "As to the purposes of the Union, therefore, Georgia is not a sovereign state;" to which may be added: and for the purposes of external sovereignty the *state* of Georgia does not exist.

If an American citizen should suffer outrage at the hands of a mob in Devonshire, or the County Cork, we should look to London for satisfaction. If an Englishman be similarly maltreated in Maine or Colorado, it is incomprehensible that Washington may not be held internationally accountable. Concede the theory of state supremacy, however, and the treaty rights of a foreigner may be grossly violated by the action or through the neglect of a state without remedy or redress—the Nation taking refuge behind the claim of state sovereignty and the state escaping because it is not an international person nor bound by the treaty. The suggestion is not fanciful. In 1880 certain Chinese, resident in Colorado, were, because of their race, brutally assaulted and murdered and their property destroyed by a mob. The Secretary of State, replying to the Chinese Minister, asserted the utter helplessness of the national government in the matter. The same thing occurred in the case of certain Italians who were the victims of mob violence in Louisiana.

But it is not true that the national government is thus powerless to vindicate its treaty obligations. Neither in the enforcement nor in the making of treaties is it limited by or dependent upon state power. It is the government of a completely sovereign Nation, possessing, in the exercise of its powers, jurisdiction over every foot of territory and direct authority over every citizen within its limits. Within the scope of its powers it may move without regard to state lines or state functionaries or state laws or constitutions, sweeping aside every obstacle sought to be interposed by individual or state authority, compelling obedience with all the powers of an unfettered hand, and answerable for what it does to the people of the Nation alone.

If the perpetrators of violence against the person and property of the foreigner living under the protection of our flag have gone unpunished, it is not from lack of power but from lack of action on the part of the national government. The power of that government is ample. It may by legislation penalize individuals who conspire to interfere with or violate, or who participate in the actual interference with, or violation, of treaty rights and privileges; it may use the army of the United States and, if necessary, call forth the state militia itself, to enforce this legislation, and preserve these rights and privileges; it may invoke the powers of the national courts to restrain violations and interferences in cases where that remedy is appropriate. In one way or in another whatever the government of the United States has the right to promise it has the power to enforce. If not, the weaknesses of the Confederation were exposed and denounced in vain; and the declared purpose of the Constitution "to form a *more perfect* Union" has failed of realization in one of its most vital phases.

CHAPTER VIII

AFTER THE WAR

The theory of governmental power which has been presented and examined in the course of the discussions now to be concluded, will grow in practical importance as we come to deal with the international problems resulting from and following the war. We have been fighting, we are told, to make the world safe for democracy, to vindicate and insure the rights of small nations, to rid the world of autocracy and put an end to military despotism. This is a recital of high and splendid aims for which to fight, but it is, nevertheless, an ideal and elusive generalization which inspires the soul without informing the understanding with any degree of precision in respect of the things which must be done to bring about its realization. It is quite obvious that a convention simply pledging the high contracting parties to keep the world safe for democracy, and free from autocracy and military despotism, and to preserve the rights of small nations, would be as fluid and unstable as the provisions of a statute commanding everybody in general terms to be good and honest under penalty of severe punishment. The fighting has come to an end and we are now confronted with the necessity of putting concrete propositions into a treaty of peace, and none of these are concrete things. Whether they shall hereafter be realized will depend not upon any fine statements of principle, but upon definite, practical, concrete stipulations, and upon the possession of power of some kind somewhere to enforce them.

Our burden of responsibility will not be ended with the signing of the treaty. In truth, it may well be, it will only then fairly begin; and it is sure to be of far-reaching scope and long continued. At the peace table we shall assist in readjusting the geography of Europe. We shall aid in formulating international policies destined to revolutionize the relationships of the civilized world. And hereafter, as long as the Nation endures, we shall never be absent from the international council chamber when great affairs are to be debated and settled. If it be unfortunate to thus finally break with the condition of splendid isolation which has hitherto been our boast and comfort, it is vain to lament the fact; for that volume of our history is closed and the new volume is opened in which to trace the record of greater achievements in broader fields. But to him who loves his country and glories in her past; who reviews with satisfaction the successive steps by which she has grown from thirteen straggling, loosely related communities of fishermen and planters and traders into forty-eight compact commonwealths knit together in one great empire with bands lighter than gossamer but more enduring than steel; who re-reads the story of devoted sacrifice by which the Union was made a definite reality, and later, and no less inspiring, that by which the oppressed subjects of an Old World power were converted into the free citizens of a New World republic, and who feels the thrill of supreme faith in her destiny of leadership and in the crystalline purity of all her motives; who believes that nations, like men, are made strong by bearing burdens and not by shirking them—to such an one the sense of these new responsibilities will come with a new sweep of exultation that his country is again afforded opportunity for service in a world where all too seldom strength and unselfishness have gone together.

This war marks the end of an old order and the beginning of a new one, as surely and in many ways as profoundly, as did the birth and life of Christ two thousand years ago. This we realized only dimly and inadequately as the vast and hideous panorama unrolled before our vision. The spiritual meaning of it all will begin to penetrate our minds only after the final adjustments of peace shall have been completed and we are able to review it in retrospect. Of all those who lived in the time of Christ, how few suspected that the world would be swept as with a flame and cleansed by the events which to them registered only the passing of a cult! The social, political, and spiritual results of the great tragedy through which we have so painfully passed will affect the destinies of mankind to an incalculable degree to the end of time. It is, therefore, certain that our own institutions will be affected, our outlook upon life profoundly altered, and our duties radically enlarged; and that, necessarily, we shall be called upon to do and participate in the doing of many things hitherto unknown in our polity.

We have for nearly a century and a half, with occasional interruptions, been like some far-off pioneer, whose relations to his neighbors—few and widely separated—are limited to the routine of periodical visits with an occasional quarrel over grazing lands or the exact location of a line fence. When he moves into town he discovers that he and his neighbors have reciprocal duties and responsibilities of every-day concern. In a similar, though larger, way we have now moved into the world of closer international relations, and shall discover that we have assumed the duties and have become entitled to the benefits of community life. Geographically, we are still bounded by the two oceans and by Canada and Mexico, except for a few outlying possessions; politically, our frontiers will hereafter be wherever our national interests and responsibilities mark them. Who could have foreseen in July, 1914, that by a series of incidents following one another and all following the assassination of an archduke at Sarajevo, we should four years later be battling to the limit of our strength upon the soil of Europe, three thousand miles across the sea? Steam and electricity and the conquest of the air have shriveled distance and brought the far places of the earth very near together, until no spot remains beyond the possibility of our interest. However remote the contingency may now seem, it is always possible that our own fate may be greatly involved in some seemingly trivial happening, half the world away.

We have many times been led by events that no human foresight could anticipate, and no human power could control; and so we may be led again. We have builded many structures which we did not ourselves design; and we may build many more. But this does not mean that we are at the mercy of blind chance. Fatalism is the doctrine of indolence and cowardice. It would be vain to deny that the movements of mankind, individually and collectively, are subject to a certain degree of constraint which they are unable to avoid. Individuals, sometimes, are swept onward by forces they are too feeble to resist. Nations, sometimes, follow currents from which they cannot escape and which they are powerless to turn aside. We are, in a sense, all of us, big and little, large nations and small, in the great stream which flows irresistibly toward unknown ports. We shall be borne upon its bosom whatever we do; but foresight will help us to avoid the rocks which ever and again loom threateningly in the channel, and skill and courage will help us through the rapids into which we shall from time to time be drawn, and bring us finally past them all to such open waters as in the wisdom and goodness of God it is intended we shall come.

In the course of the adventurous voyage upon which we are embarked we have reached the point where we must sail in closer contact with other ships of the fleet. In other words, the period of national detachment has ended and that of international coöperation has supervened. The other nations with whom we shall coöperate will want to know, and will have a right to know, not only the things we think should be included in the new order, but what we are willing and able to do upon our part toward their consummation. We have become too closely and vitally involved in the tangle of international problems to any longer, or ever again, stand apart. It would not only be a great embarrassment, but a great misfortune, if it should transpire that there is anything which we ought but which, for lack of constitutional power, we are unable to do. The importance

of conceding to the national government the full measure of power which it has been the main purpose of the
preceding discussions to sustain, is clearly apparent.
The time is fast approaching, if it be not already here,
when we must be able to assert and maintain for that
government the unimpaired powers of complete external sovereignty. We must not—we cannot—enter upon
this field of amplified activity with half-developed limbs.
The complete powers of the governments of other nations must be matched by the complete powers of our
own government. Upon this enlarged stage of international negotiation and coöperation we cannot afford
to play the part of a political cripple. Our government
must come to its new tasks not only with full, but with
unquestioned powers. To be obliged to confess, when
called upon to deal with some novel but vital matter,
that the government lacked sufficient authority, because of the absence of affirmative language in the
Constitution, would be most humiliating and regret-
table; and to find the power only after a microscopic
search of that instrument, and a strained or doubtful
interpretation of its words, would be almost as unfortunate. Any theory of constitutional construction
which leads to such a result will not bear analysis and
must be rejected.

The task of the soldier is finished and that of the
statesman—less bloody but no less difficult—has begun.
The war has answered many questions, but it has asked
and will ask more than it has answered. The precise
nature of many of these interrogatories lies in the womb
of the future, beyond the wisdom of the wisest to fore-
know; but the reply may affect us for good or ill for all

time. It does not now, for example, seem probable that we shall ever acquire territory or be called upon to exercise governmental control anywhere on the Eastern continent, but in the light of our acquisition of the Philippines, who can undertake to deny the possibility of even such a contingency as this? However that may be, it is certain that we shall feel the weight of our extra-territorial responsibilities in many unaccustomed ways. In this broadened field of endeavor we must cease to think in terms of states and states' rights and think only in terms of nationality. We must cease to measure the authority of the general government only by what the Constitution affirmatively grants, and consider it also in the light of what the Constitution permits from failure to deny. There is no danger that we shall thereby destroy the reserved rights of the states, or overrun the domain of local government—against these unfortunate consequences we must always be on our guard—but we shall avoid the unspeakably absurd confusion of having an agency to speak for us upon all matters of legitimate international concern with a vocabulary so limited that upon some of them—and, in the light of our expanded world relations, not inconceivably the most vital of them—it cannot speak at all.

While it is impossible to anticipate all the external problems with which we shall hereafter be called upon to deal, some of them lie very clearly before us. First and most important is that of the public defense. We have been in the habit of expressing our hopes by saying that this was a war to end war; and there are some who have convinced themselves that, it having been won by the Allied nations, the world will enter upon an era of everlasting peace. That the complete overthrow of the Central Powers will be followed by an indefinitely long-continued period of peace is most likely, but that war will never again be waged is a conclusion not only without substantial warrant, but one the indulgence of which will constitute for us a seriously dangerous delusion. The causes of war among nations and peoples lie very deep in the nature of mankind—far deeper than armaments or land hunger or kings or capitalists or forms of government. Like the impulses to sin they are protean, but unlike these they frequently spring from sentiments of the most sacredly justifying character. Man is a fighting animal, and in the last analysis, in response to emotions stronger than himself, will fight for the things he holds dear. The fighting spirit is one which it is to be hoped we shall never lose; for directed along right channels it is as necessary as the spirit of peace. It is not enough for a nation to *desire* justice, it must have the will and, when needed, the power to enforce it. As time goes on, war between nations will become less and less frequent. So much is indicated by the course of past history; but the same history demonstrates that forces are at work in the world stronger than the desires of any portion of humanity—forces that generally do not, and generally will not, succeed in driving us out of the paths of peace, but which now and then have swept, and will again, sometimes, sweep us with a tempest of passion into the chaos of war. It is right that we should teach the desirability of peace, and that we should teach it intensely and continuously; but we should, at the same time, keep before ourselves always the clear danger of war, and at our peril be prepared to meet it. Not to do so is to dwell in the same fool's paradise which is occupied by the individual who imagines that he can always maintain his rights and his comfort without effort on his own part to do so. The dove is a pacifist; the eagle is not. The dove falls a victim to rapacity; the eagle is immune—not because of their differing views on the subject of pacifism but because one is weak and timid and the other is strong and self-reliant. And it is not the dove, let me remind you, but the eagle which symbolizes the spirit of America: Yield nothing to the aggressor! A nation, like a man, must carefully distinguish between the desire for peace which springs from a timid soul, anxious only to be safe, and that which comes from a stout heart seeking the way of righteousness. There are two kinds of men, equally detestable: he who seeks a fight because he is a bully, and he who avoids a fight because he is a coward. As with a man, so with a nation, the course of wisdom and rectitude is neither to seek nor run away from a conflict but to stand. If I were able to transcend the limitations of time and anticipate the final verdict of history upon my countrymen, I would have it written in words of everlasting light: *They respected the liberties of others because they were just, and kept their own because they were strong and resolute.*

Let us not permit our judgment to be unduly influenced by our desires. We are still a long way from that millennium of the poet's vision which is to witness the permanent retirement of the war drum and the battle flag; and until that long-desired and blessed event shall have come to pass, it will be well for us to shape our course upon the theory that in our intercourse with other nations days of stress are sure to come, when the grim *semper paratus* of our battleships and armies, as of old, will be more effective than a soft answer to turn away wrath. The freeman's peace is something more than the absence of war. A state of war is always dreadful, but it is a sweet and holy thing compared with a peace of ignoble capitulation to wrong. No properly constituted man loves war for its own sake but, sometimes,

> "He needs must fight
> To make true peace his own;
> He needs must combat might with might,
> Or might would rule alone."

And this, being granted, necessarily establishes the wisdom of a policy of military readiness, in order that a true peace may be made more certain of attainment.

Preparedness for national defense is not confined to military preparation alone, though obviously that is a matter of chief importance for which there is no substitute. In addition, however, there is need of that intellectual and spiritual training which will bring to the individual a clear comprehension of the nature and quality of our institutions, and an abiding sense of the importance of their protection against destructive or deteriorating assaults on the part of enemies from without or from within our borders. It is highly desirable that we should keep alive the new spirit of nationalism, which has been born of the war, and which is fast fusing the heterogeneous groups of German-Americans and Irish-Americans and other hyphenated tribal collections into a homogeneous body of American citizens who are for the first time beginning to realize their essential unity. If no other benefit should result from the dreadful struggle, the firm establishment of this new spirit of national concord would justify every sacrifice we have made, or might have been called upon to make, however terrible; for it is certain that only thus have we been brought to an understanding of, and a deliverance from, the sinister peril of a divided allegiance which threatened our very existence as a separate and independent people.

The false doctrine that patriotism is a narrow and provincial trait incompatible with our duty to mankind in general should never again be permitted to go without vigorous challenge. Patriotism is something far older than our institutions and far stronger than any impulse to individual preservation; for men in all ages have willingly sacrificed themselves in untold numbers in response to its appeal. It is the sentiment which binds the people of a country together for the common good and the common defense, without which they would perish; and so clearly necessary is it to their continued existence as an independent unit of society that if it were not an instinctive attribute of the soul, it would be necessary to develop it by artificial means.

That form of internationalism which teaches that the stranger beyond our gates should be the object of our solicitude equally with the loved, mutually helpful members of our own household is not sound sentiment but maudlin sentimentality. The form of internationalism in which I believe is that of cordial coöperation among nations for the welfare and betterment of the people of all lands, but which will always look first to the welfare and betterment of our own. The more scrupulously we care for our own, the more strongly will they be disposed to care for others. A helping hand is like the quality of mercy—"it is twice blessed, it blesses him that gives and him that takes;" and a people blessed with receiving much will not forego the blessing which comes from giving much. But it would mean very little to be an American if a thin fondness for all the tribes of men should be substituted for that passionate love of country and that flaming devotion to her flag, which brought the flower of the Nation to the sacrificial fields of France as to a place of great privilege.

There is also a material preparedness which it will be perilous to neglect. The war has taught us, as we have never been taught before, the necessity of building up and rendering permanently dependable our material resources, so that we may be entirely independent of other countries for all necessary supplies in time of war. It not only must never be possible for any other nation to suspend above our heads the dreadful menace of starvation, which hung suspended for so many anxious weeks above Great Britain while the submarine was gaining upon the shipyard; but it must never be possible for us to be deprived of any necessary or useful commodity, if from any cause its importation shall be prevented. To increase the output of our products in all the fields of industry, and make secure its continuance by reasonable and fostering legislation is not only wise economic policy in time of peace but may prove a bulwark of defense in time of war.

But spiritual and material preparation will be of little avail against the evil consequences of war without military preparedness as well; and even the addition of military preparedness will not suffice unless it be thoroughgoing. If Great Britain in 1914 had been able to mobilize a great army as quickly as she was able to mobilize her great navy, either there would have been no war or it would quickly have been over. If we had done our duty in the past instead of grossly neglecting it, and had been able to put one out of every twenty of our population into the fighting line as readily as Switzerland is able to put one out of every ten of her population into the fighting line, either we should have had no occasion to enter the war, or it would have been victoriously won long ago. Rather than to misplace our dependence in the protection of a feeble military establishment, it were better to have none, but to rely wholly on that kindly providence which is supposed to preserve the fool from the logical consequences of his folly.

The first requisite of military preparedness is an adequate navy. While it is true that the absence of an adequate English army probably precipitated the war, and undoubtedly prolonged it, it is no less true that only the strength and readiness of the British navy prevented the war from resulting in the subjugation of Europe. For three years it was literally true that the battleships of Great Britain stood between the democratic world, ourselves included, and supreme disaster. That risk we must never incur again. With rich and vulnerable coasts fronting on the two oceans, easily open to attack or invasion, it is little short of criminal folly to leave them without the most adequate protection. The navy as the first line of defense should be

maintained at such a degree of power and efficiency as
to furnish a fleet for the Atlantic and a fleet for the
Pacific, each sufficiently powerful to afford protection
against attack without the aid of the other; for we
must not be unprepared for the contingency of a combination of European and Asiatic powers against us.
The bitter lesson of this war is that military strength
cannot be improvised, and we should not again permit
ourselves to be lulled into a false sense of security by
the fatuous suggestion of a million citizens springing to
arms over night—a suggestion which might have been
substantial if only the citizens had been taught to
spring, and provision had first been made to have the
arms within reasonable springing distance.

We must strengthen the coast fortifications we already have at critical points and construct others
wherever needed, and maintain them all at the highest
level of efficiency with guns which in range and power
keep pace with the latest and best expressions of military science. The personnel of the coast artillery until
recently has been shamefully and dangerously below
the most meager limit of necessity, a situation whose
existence we cannot afford to permit again; for it is
useless to have guns, however perfect, without expert
gunners to use them. The coast artilleryman has a
greater degree of technical training than any other man
in the military service. It has been of such character
that in case of need he may serve with the field artillery,
the machine guns, or the infantry, or in any service
where a working knowledge of electric appliances may
be needed. There is no danger of having an over-
supply of these highly efficient men.

The third line of defense is the army. It is impossible to deal with the subject as fully as its importance warrants and what I have to say must necessarily be compressed into a few sentences. A large professional army is not desirable for several reasons, among them that it takes too many from the productive employments and is a heavy burden of expense. It will be sufficient for us to provide for, and maintain on a peace footing, a regular army of from 300,000 to 500,000 men, fully equipped with the latest and best military appliances, and trained and kept trained to the highest point of modern efficiency. These men should be maintained at fewer places and in larger numbers than has hitherto been the case, and to this end we should abandon most of the small forts scattered about the country, and retain only such of them as occupy positions of strategical value for concentration and like purposes. These forts, each capable of accommodating a few hundred troops, were in the main established at a time when it was necessary to have small bodies of soldiers at widely separated points, so as to be readily available for the quick suppression of Indian uprisings. That situation no longer exists, and hereafter the use of military forces is likely to be in large bodies, which in order to operate effectively in time of war must be accustomed to acting together in time of peace.

Such an army, however, is only a vanguard and will prove altogether insufficient for our needs in any defensive warfare we are likely to be called upon to wage— and it is greatly to be hoped that occasion for any other kind will not arise—for it is clear that only a very strong military power, or a combination of powers, will ever assume the risk of attacking us. But a rich nation like ourselves, ambitious for commercial expansion, will inevitably run counter to the ambitions of other people and invite animosities which may easily develop into acts of aggression unless it be known that we are prepared to overcome force with greater force. To that end we should adopt and hereafter maintain a thoroughgoing system of universal compulsory military training. We should begin with our boys when they reach the age of fourteen years by imposing as part of their regular school work such physical training as will develop their strength—together with a ready ability to use it —their courage, self-reliance, and power of initiative. An admirable foundation upon which to build this system is that afforded by the principles of the boy scout movement. When these boys reach the age of seventeen years their military training should begin and continue intensively for a period of three years. Either the Swiss or the Australian system may be profitably adopted and under either system not more than an average of two months each year need be taken for this purpose. This will not interfere with the education of the young men nor their usefulness in the ordinary pursuits of life. The result will be that in a few years we shall have a potential military force of many millions, who can be mobilized and made ready for active service in a few weeks. This training should be under the general direction and exclusive control of the national government. The state militia has never been a really dependable national military asset, and we should not carry its disturbing principles into the field of universal military training.

It is a mistake to suppose that such a system would render war more likely. As the Swiss experience has demonstrated, it will, on the contrary, constitute a very powerful influence for peace. Surely we have by this time discovered that it is weakness, and not strength, which invites attack. There is no more danger that a body of men pursuing the vocations of peace will be likely to favor an offensive war because they know how to fight than there is that a single individual will be quarrelsome because he is strong, courageous, and self-reliant.

With such a navy, with such protected coasts, and with such an army, backed by such a body of trained citizens, we could not only put behind us all fear of invasion or successful attack from any power, or any possible combination of powers but, at the same time, have a more virile and capable population for the development of all the arts of peace. To those whose hearts sink at the thought of the expense of such a program it is sufficient to say that the prevention of a single great war in fifty years would alone justify it. We have spent more money in the past eighteen months to reach a degree of preparedness sufficient to enable us to render effective assistance to our powerful allies than it would have cost us during the entire period since the Civil War to maintain a military establishment of the character outlined, and of a progressive strength relatively proportioned to our changing necessities.

Universal military training is essentially democratic —primitively democratic; for in the days of our forefathers every man was a fighting man trained in the school of every-day experience. His rifle and powder-

horn hung upon the wall ready for instant use. Our
young men no longer obtain skill in the use of weapons
by daily contact with the hard problems of frontier life;
and there is, therefore, need of stimulated training unless we are content to become a race of weaklings and
ultimately suffer the penalty of conquest and perhaps
domination at the hands of some hardier race. If it
be wise for a democracy to acquire sufficient intelli-
gence to vote for the establishment and maintenance
of free institutions, surely it is no less wise for them to
learn how to defend and preserve these institutions
from destruction. Even those who are opposed to
military preparedness do not question the right of the
people to fight in their own defense, only they seem to
think that there is some mysterious virtue in not being
able to fight well.

Let us rid ourselves of the superstition that militarism is a mere matter of armies and navies. Every
man in Switzerland is a soldier; France not only com-
pels universal training, but universal service; Great
Britain has a navy far exceeding in power any other in
the world; but militarism curses none of these countries. Militarism is a spirit—that false and evil spirit
of force which teaches that right and justice may ask
no questions of might. A great army may be the instrument of militarism as a facile tongue may be the
instrument for the utterance of a lie, but the lie itself
is of the spirit and not of the tongue. It is as false to
say that armies and navies necessarily produce militarism as it would be to say that a tongue necessarily
makes its possessor a liar.

The subject of preparedness cannot be dismissed without some reference—necessarily brief—to the suggested plan for a League of Nations to enforce peace.

Peace is so desirable and war so dreadful that any proposal which promises a peaceful substitute for warfare in the settlement of international disputes immediately enlists our sympathies and makes a well-nigh irresistible appeal for our support. For this very reason we must be on our guard, lest by lending a too-willing ear to the plausible but impracticable we permit our judgment to be betrayed by our desire.

The world has grown to a condition of vast complexity with a multitude of diverse and conflicting interests. Some nations have all the territory they wish and are anxious only to be left undisturbed. Such is the case of Great Britain; such is our own case. Other nations living in cramped quarters are land hungry, and long for expansion. Such was the case of Germany; such is the case of Japan. The pressure for an outlet for the surplus populations of growing countries of limited area is not likely to become less, and will always constitute a possible incitement to warlike aggression. There is the problem of the uncivilized and the partially civilized races; the problem of the small and the submerged nationalities, and a vast number of other problems which have vexed humanity from the beginning, and are not likely to be eliminated in the near future. It is greatly to be desired that some feasible method should be devised for a peaceful determination of international disputes arising out of these and similar conditions whenever they become acute; but the method must be practicable as well as righteous. We would better endure the ills we have than accept any plan, however alluring, whose highly probable failure would result in a revival of the old conditions in perhaps an intensified and more stubborn form. It is pre-eminently a time and situation for the sort of action which will take us forward securely, even if slowly, rather than to a doubtful ending in great haste. I think, therefore, we shall, in the long run, secure better and more lasting results by a gradual extension of the principles and plans already initiated by The Hague Conferences than by adopting the more ambitious and more adventurous plan now suggested for the League of Nations, including as its distinguishing feature the use of some form of international force. Few countries were ready for such a plan before the war, and there is grave danger that any radical provision for peace enforcement adopted under the present tense and excited condition of world thought will be found unworkable after we shall have returned to a normal state of mind.

We are told that as the use of force is necessary and potent to maintain peace among individuals it is necessary and will be potent in the case of nations; but inferences drawn from analogies are sometimes deceptive. Because we may agree that the conduct of an individual and the conduct of a nation should be governed by the same moral standards, it does not follow that identical measures of enforcement or of punishment will be equally successful or applicable. The guilt of the individual is purely personal; but in the case of national misbehavior the people are seldom equally culpable, and often a large proportion of them are not culpable at all. To use military force against a nation by way of coercion or punishment is, therefore, to inflict suffering indiscriminately upon the guilty and the innocent alike, a wrong which constitutes one of the principal injustices of war and ought not to be deliberately perpetuated in a scheme of international justice designed to put an end to war. The plan really involves a military combination pledged to make war upon any member of the League who begins hostilities against another member without first submitting the dispute to arbitration. It is not proposed at present, as I understand, to enforce the arbitral decree by the use of military force, though it does not seem illogical to conclude that such an extension of the proposal must inevitably follow. It is this feature of the plan, thought by some to be its principal strength, which I am persuaded will prove its fatal weakness.

In the first place, it is not always easy to determine who is responsible for commencing hostilities. There is in modern diplomacy a good deal of skillful and disingenuous maneuvering on the part of each of the antagonists to put the other in the attitude of beginning the war, and this practice would undoubtedly be accentuated under conditions where the aggressor would be placed at a serious disadvantage by incurring the armed opposition of the League. It is vain to imagine that the formation of the League would put an end to the antagonisms which divide some nations, and the common interests which unite others. Common ideals, common language, common interests, a thousand unforeseeable causes, will still tend to bind nations together, and an opposite state of affairs to hold them apart. It is reasonable to suppose, therefore, that in determining the question of culpability an unbiased opinion will never be certain. Sooner or later a case will arise where an attempt to use the international forces against one party or the other will meet with internal resistance so serious that either the attempt will be abandoned or something resembling civil war among the members of the League will supervene. In the former event the experiment would fail ingloriously, and in the latter event, ingloriously and disastrously; and because of the magnitude of the interests involved the failure would arrest the movement in the direction of world coöperation for peace for many years to come.

The factors are so many and complex, the crosscurrents of international interests so varied, the views of the advocates of the plan respecting the control, formation, and character of the military forces to be employed, and the nature of the administrative machinery to be adopted, so indefinite as to surround the entire proposal with an atmosphere of the gravest doubt.

How is the power of the League to be distributed? How is its administration to be constituted? How are the military forces to be made up and under what direction are they to be operated? If we bind ourselves to join with other nations in raising and equipping military forces to coerce and punish rebellious and disobedient members of the League by making war upon them whenever the governing agency of the League shall so determine, what will happen in the not impossible event that the sympathies of our people are with the recalcitrant member—as, for example, in a controversy between France and Germany, with France in the rôle of aggressor—and Congress, vested with the power to declare war and appropriate moneys, should refuse to act?

These and other questions admonish us against relying too unreservedly upon any experimental plan for ending international warfare; and to rely upon any such plan as a substitute for our own strength and readiness would, in my judgment, be the utmost reach of folly. There is today throughout the world an overwhelming sense of war weariness; but that will pass away and newer sensations will come with the problems of another day, and it is for that later day and not for this, that we must take heed.

More satisfactory results, it seems to me, are to be obtained by following and extending the principles already enunciated by The Hague Conferences. Great and valuable progress has already been made. There has been a constantly growing disposition to submit international differences to arbitration. Certain weaknesses, however, should be eliminated and extension made in two directions: (1) by broadening the scope of the jurisdiction, and (2) by substituting for the present arbitral tribunal a real international court with judicial power.

1. Provision should be made for submitting all questions of a justiciable nature by reason of their being susceptible of decision by the application of the principles of law or equity. In other words, the jurisdictional test furnished by the unratified treaties of the Taft administration should be adopted. As already pointed out, the exception of cases involving questions of honor and vital interests is not only unnecessary but

mischievous. The reasons for this conclusion have already been stated in Chapter VI and need not be repeated.

The constitution and practice of our own National Supreme Court furnish striking and sufficient proof of the entire feasibility of the suggested test. The distinction between judicial questions which the Court has power to determine, and political questions which the Court refuses to entertain, has been clearly established.

2. The great weakness of the present plan is that international controversies are submitted not to a court bound by legal rules, but to a board of arbitrators selected by the opposing parties and who, therefore, enter upon the trial of the cause not as so many judges but as so many advocates. The tendency of such a proceeding is, therefore, to bring about a judgment for one side or the other, not according to strict right, but a compromise more or less unfair and unsatisfactory to both sides. In the place of this tribunal there is no reason why we should not, as our government has heretofore insisted, provide for a judicial court of justice whose members shall be selected for their learning, integrity, and ability, and whose tenure of office and compensation shall be sufficient to induce men of the requisite ability and character to serve to the exclusion of all other occupation. No better model for the establishment of such a Court can be found than that furnished by the Supreme Court of the United States, which has been vested with jurisdiction over controversies between different states of the Union. The signatories of the convention should agree to submit all controversies falling within the description of the juris-

dictional clause, to this tribunal for decision, and should bind themselves explicitly to abide by its determination. It will be neither advisable nor necessary to employ military forces to put the decrees of such a Court into effect. The force of public opinion throughout the world will be sufficient to insure compliance, as it has been sufficient thus far to insure compliance with the numerous decrees rendered under the process of arbitration. The problem is not so much to secure obedience to the decree of an international tribunal, as it is to secure the consent of the various nations to the establishment of the tribunal and common agreement respecting its constitution and powers. In spite of the cynical indifference of the late German government toward the "opinions of mankind," and, indeed, largely because of that attitude, the nations, and particularly the great nations, in the future, will be more than ever amenable to their compelling force.

Eighty-six years ago Andrew Jackson could, with impunity, defy a decision of the Supreme Court of the United States, constraining the action of a "sovereign" state; but any President who should attempt to do that today would be overwhelmed by the storm of popular disapproval which would ensue. Public confidence in and reverence for that great Court have become so firmly established that no state against whom an adverse decision were rendered would dream of opposing or withholding compliance with it. That an army should be utilized or should be necessary to enforce such a decision is simply unthinkable.

Popular government means self-restraint, and that leaven, since Andrew Jackson's day, has been at work

silently, but with great power, until the free people of
the earth have come to an intelligent comprehension
of the truth that liberty can never survive the destruction of order; and order perishes whenever the judg-
ments of the established courts of justice do not command ready and respectful obedience. It is, therefore,
reasonable to expect there would be, or would speedily
develop, on the part of the civilized world, a sentiment
of respect for and confidence in the decisions of an
International Court of Justice, so powerful as to
threaten any non-complying nation with international
outlawry and render compliance a simple matter of
course. At any rate, if the world has not advanced to
such a period of respect for law and order among nations as to insure this result, it has not reached the
point where it may safely rely upon its own enduring
adherence to any other plan of peace enforcement.

INDEX

COLUMBIA UNIVERSITY LECTURES

CARPENTIER LECTURES

The Nature and Sources of the Law. By JOHN CHIPMAN GRAY, LL.D., Royall Professor of Law in Harvard University. 12mo, cloth, pp. xii + 332. Price, $1.50 *net*.

World Organization as Affected by the Nature of the Modern State. By HON. DAVID JAYNE HILL, sometime American Ambassador to Germany. 12mo, cloth, pp. ix + 214. Price, $1.50 *net*.

The Genius of the Common Law. By the RT. HON. SIR FREDERICK POLLOCK, Bart., D.C.L., LL.D., Bencher of Lincoln's Inn, Barrister-at-Law. 12mo, cloth, pp. vii + 141. Price, $1.50 *net*.

The Mechanics of Law Making. By COURTENAY ILBERT, G.C.B., Clerk of the House of Commons. 12mo, cloth, pp. viii + 209. Price, $1.50 *net*.

HEWITT LECTURES

The Problem of Monopoly. By JOHN BATES CLARK, LL.D., Professor of Political Economy, Columbia University. 12mo, cloth, pp. vi + 128. Price, $1.25 *net*.

Power. By CHARLES EDWARD LUCKE, PH.D., Professor of Mechanical Engineering, Columbia University. 12mo, cloth, pp. vii + 316. Illustrated. Price, $2.00 *net*.

The Doctrine of Evolution. Its Basis and its Scope. By HENRY EDWARD CRAMPTON, PH.D., Professor of Zoology, Columbia University. 12mo, cloth, pp. ix + 311. Price, $1.50 *net*.

Medieval Story and the Beginnings of the Social Ideals of English-Speaking People. By WILLIAM WITHERLE LAWRENCE, PH.D., Associate Professor of English, Columbia University. 12mo, cloth, pp. xiv + 236. Price, $1.50 *net*.

Law and its Administration. By HARLAN F. STONE, LL.D., Dean of the School of Law, Columbia University. 12mo, cloth, pp. vii + 232. Price. $1.50 *net*.

American City Progress and the Law. By HOWARD LEE McBAIN, PH.D., Professor of Municipal Science and Administration, Columbia University. 12mo, cloth, pp. viii + 269. Price, $1.50 *net*.

JESUP LECTURES

Light. By RICHARD C. MACLAURIN, LL.D., ScD., President of the Massachusetts Institute of Technology. 12mo, cloth, pp. ix + 251. Portrait and figures. Price, $1.50 *net*.

COLUMBIA UNIVERSITY PRESS
LEMCKE & BUECHNER, *Agents*
30–32 EAST 20TH STREET, NEW YORK

COLUMBIA UNIVERSITY LECTURES

JESUP LECTURES

Scientific Features of Modern Medicine. By FREDERIC S. LEE, PH.D., Dalton Professor of Physiology, Columbia University. 12mo, cloth, pp. vii + 183. Price, $1.50 *net*.

Heredity and Sex. By THOMAS HUNT MORGAN, PH.D., Professor of Experimental Zoology in Columbia University. Second edition. 12mo, cloth, pp. ix + 284. Illustrated. Price, $1.75 *net*.

Dynamic Psychology. By ROBERT SESSIONS WOODWORTH, PH.D., Professor of Psychology, Columbia University. 12mo, cloth, pp. ix + 210. Price, $1.50 *net*.

MUNICIPAL GOVERNMENT

The Government of Municipalities. By DORMAN B. EATON. 8vo, cloth, pp. x + 498 + 28. $4.00 *net*.

Municipal Home Rule. A Study in Administration. By FRANK J. GOODNOW, LL.D., President of Johns Hopkins University. 12mo, cloth, pp. xxiv + 283. $1.50 *net*.

Municipal Problems. By FRANK J. GOODNOW, LL.D., President of Johns Hopkins University. 12mo, cloth, pp. xiii+321. $1.50 *net*.

The Law and the Practice of Municipal Home Rule. By HOWARD LEE McBAIN, PH.D., Professor of Municipal Science and Administration, Columbia University. 8vo, cloth, pp. xviii + 724. $5.00 *net*.

Four Stages of Greek Religion. By GILBERT MURRAY, Regius Professor of Greek, in the University of Oxford. 8vo, cloth, pp. 223. Price, $1.50 *net*.

Lectures on Science, Philosophy, and Art. A series of twenty-one lectures descriptive in non-technical language of the achievements in Science, Philosophy, and Art. 8vo, cloth. Price, $5.00 *net*.

Greek Literature. A series of ten lectures delivered at Columbia University by scholars from various universities. 8vo, cloth, pp. vii + 306. Price, $2.00 *net*.

COLUMBIA UNIVERSITY PRESS
LEMCKE & BUECHNER, *Agents*
30–32 EAST 20TH STREET, NEW YORK